Land of Destiny

A History of Vancouver Real Estate

JESSE DONALDSON

Anvil Press • Vancouver

Anvil Press Publishers Inc.
PO Box 3008, Main Post Office
Vancouver, BC V6B 3X5 Canada

Library and Archives Canada Cataloguing in Publication

Title: Land of destiny : a history of Vancouver real estate / by Jesse Donaldson.
Names: Donaldson, Jesse, 1982- author.
Description: First edition. | Series statement: 49.2 : tales from the offbeat ; #1
Identifiers: Canadiana 20190165677 | ISBN 9781772141443 (softcover)
Subjects: LCSH: Real estate business—British Columbia—Vancouver—History. | LCSH: Housing—British Columbia—Vancouver—History. | LCSH: Housing policy—British Columbia—Vancouver—History.
Classification: LCC HD320.V3 D66 2019 | DDC 333.309711/33—dc23

Book design by Clint Hutzulak/Rayola.com
Author photo by Albert Nicholas Photography
Represented in Canada by Publishers Group Canada
Distributed by Raincoast Books

The publisher gratefully acknowledges the financial assistance of the Canada Council for the Arts, the Canada Book Fund, and the Province of British Columbia through the BC Arts Council and the Book Publishing Tax Credit.

Printed and bound in Canada

CONTENTS

"Oh! Sad is the fate of Vancouver,
  Its sweet little game's about over,
  I said from the first,
  The bubble would burst
  And astonish the dupes of Vancouver"

— ***Port Moody Gazette***, August 28, 1886

STARTS

"Vancouver is facing a housing crisis."

So wrote the *Vancouver News-Herald* in April of 1941.

It wasn't the first time the phrase saw print, and of course, it wouldn't be the last. For Vancouverites alive today, there has never been a time when affordability (or more precisely, the lack thereof) wasn't a regular topic of conversation — at parties, on social media, and on the front page of our few remaining newspapers. As of 2019, there isn't a single rental suite in the city that is affordable to an employee making minimum wage. The rental vacancy rate sits at 0.8% — among the lowest in history. There isn't a detached home on the market selling for less than one million dollars, and the average house costs ten to twenty times the annual average salary. The gap between investors and working Vancouverites is stark: forty-six per cent of the city's condominiums are investor-owned, while close to a quarter of households identified as being in "core housing need" (meaning they spend more than one-third of their income on shelter). Between 2002 and 2016, the average price of a detached home went from four-hundred thousand dollars to almost two million dollars, while incomes have remained stagnant. The city's current challenges are hardly unique; affordability is of grave concern in jurisdictions around the world. What sets Vancouver apart are its generally low wages, and an economy virtually dependent on development cash. In mid-2017, *Mother Jones* described the city as a global cautionary tale, noting that "the Vancouver debacle should be a required case study for urban politicians, activists, and citizens everywhere," and less than a year later, *Macleans*' Terry Glavin called it "a global swindler's paradise for real estate racketeering, a city that is now also one of the world's most hopelessly pathetic urban landscapes of housing affordability."

How did this happen? Who is responsible? Was this avoidable? Inevitable? An unfortunate accident? As it turns out, it's been happening for decades. And it was anything but an accident. In fact, the current state of the housing market has been more than one-hundred years in the making.

Before Vancouver was a city, it was — first and foremost — a real estate investment.

Even predating its incorporation in 1886, real estate has always been the city's most valuable resource and its most prominent industry, and over the past 130 years, that industry has shaped virtually every aspect of Vancouver's growth — from its name, to its placement in Coal Harbour, to the names of its most prominent streets and neighbourhoods, to the creation of its local landmarks (including Stanley Park, Science World, False Creek, and Olympic Village), to its involvement in global cultural and sporting events like Expo '86 and the 2010 Olympics. Simply put, the history of Vancouver is the history of real estate, a history written by men (and yes, they're mostly men) whose names might sound familiar — people like Jack Poole, Gordon Campbell, and Victor Li — but it's also the work of men and women whose names have faded from recent memory, people like Arthur Wellington Ross and Walter Gravely, Larry Killam, and Gerald Sutton Brown.

The history of Vancouver is the history of real estate. By 1887, less than a year after incorporation, the city had twelve grocery stores and sixteen real estate firms. By 1911, there was one real estate agent for every 150 people. The city has always been a speculator's wet dream — attracting investors like Rudyard Kipling and J.D. Rockefeller — and successive civic and provincial governments have managed this using different approaches — from the inspired to the insane.

The history of Vancouver is the history of real estate.

But, like it or not, the business model of the real estate industry is — and always has been — displacement for the sake of profit, which means that, more than anything else, the history of Vancouver is a history of displacement. It's a history of speculation, of property being appropriated, bought, swapped, and hyper-inflated by a moneyed class that's often part of the global financial elite, and the arguments that persist today — about exorbitant prices, about non-existent vacancy rates, about global speculation, about systemic corruption, about government malfeasance, about haves and have-nots — are simply the continuation of more than 130 years of real estate oligarchy. Of course, those doing the speculating and development have changed, but ultimately, it doesn't matter if it was the CPR in 1884 or Concord Pacific in 1986. Our current state of affairs is the result of a deliberate, century-long campaign on the part of wealthy development interests — and their enablers in government — to increase profits and line their pockets, one that regards ordinary, working Vancouverites as little more than collateral damage.

Today, one-third of BC's GDP is related in some way to the real estate sector, and as such, developers and the people who finance them occupy every conceivable position within the halls of power. Until 2017, condominium marketer Bob Rennie was both the primary backer for Vision Vancouver, and the chief fundraiser for the reigning BC Liberal party. Gordon Campbell, Vancouver's mayor and BC's premier for more than a decade, financed virtually his entire political career with development industry money. Make no mistake: any slowing of the development or construction sectors would be catastrophic for the provincial economy. But the impact of the development community's more than one hundred years of hegemony have themselves been catastrophic.

Can it be fixed? Are we doomed? Sometimes the best way forward is by first looking back. To recognize the patterns history provides us, to explore the paths others have taken when presented with similar circumstances. To dodge mistakes and emulate successes. Examining the city through the lens of its most prominent industry, the similarities between past and present are sometimes astonishing, often sobering, and regularly fascinating.

Before Vancouver was a city, it was — first and foremost — a real estate investment.

Some things haven't changed.

GREEN
(1884 – 1913)

*"Land prices are high, it is said, higher than
anything would warrant. 'Why, the workingmen
cannot afford to pay at the rate demanded for
these tiny outside lots,' asserted one man
recently. The same thing was said here 20 years
ago, answer the pioneers; others of us know
that it was repeated 10 years ago and five years
ago, and our children and our children's children
will hear the same tale of woe decades hence."*

— **R.J. McDougall,** ***BC Magazine,*** **1911**

1.

THE LETTER

*"Four hundred well-developed pines, a few
thousand tons of granite scattered in blocks,
and a sprinkling of earth. That's a town lot in
Vancouver. You order your agent to hold it until
property rises, then sell out and buy more land
further out of town [...] I do not quite see how
this helps the growth of the town [...] but it is
the essence of speculation."*

— Rudyard Kipling, 1889

ONE AFTERNOON in the spring of 1884, Walter Gravely received a
visitor.

"He came to me one day with a letter," Gravely later recalled. "He
made me promise that, whether or no [sic] the contents of it led to
business, I would tell no one of its contents."

"He" was Arthur Wellington Ross. That Ross would be arriving

with a letter wasn't unusual; he often served as the de facto postman
for the townsite of Granville, lugging the mail bag down from the
Hastings Mill, and dumping its contents on the counter of the nearby
Granville Hotel. But like Gravely, Ross was also a real estate speculator; the two men had met in Winnipeg during the early 1880s, where
they — among others — had made a fortune buying and flipping
properties in advance of the arrival of the Canadian Pacific Railway.
Briefly, Ross had been one of Winnipeg's richest citizens, having
formed a syndicate in 1881 with the express purpose of speculating
during the resultant land boom. Unfortunately, while Gravely managed to walk away during the inevitable bust that followed, moving
west with two thousand dollars in his pocket, Ross — like many of
the investors he had lured in with the promise of riches — was left
penniless. A barrel-chested Scotsman with a full head of hair and a
thick beard, Ross had always played fast and loose with money —
most of it belonging to others. Over the course of his brief time in
Winnipeg, he had made (and lost) more than most people saw in a
lifetime. Much of his success during the Winnipeg boom had come
from his willingness to play both sides; as a federal MP for the riding
of Lisgar, he regularly used inside information from the Dominion
Land Office for his own personal gain, leading the deputy minister of
the interior to later remark, in an exasperated letter: "Having the
inside track in this way, they were able, on every occasion of receipt of
a list of Half Breed allotments to be on the spot at the right time, to
their own great advantage, and the disadvantage of all other speculators in the same class of claims." The *Manitoba Free Press* was even less
charitable in its assessment of Ross' character, describing him as "an
ultra specimen of that class of men, all too numerous in Canada, who
seek public confidence and position that they may use them, not for
the gratification of a worthy ambition, in distinguishing themselves
by noble deeds and patriotic achievements, but for securing their
own most essentially selfish ends."

And by the spring of 1884, Ross had a new ally in his never-ending quest for profit; in addition to having the inside track on Crown land, he was now in the pocket of the most influential corporation in Canada: the CPR. Initially an opponent of the railroad, Ross had recently fled Winnipeg amidst a storm of controversy, after making a sudden — and suspicious — about-face in parliament. His finances in shambles after the Winnipeg bust, Ross suddenly became a staunch champion of the CPR, in one instance even voting for the company's interests over the wishes of his own constituents (an act which led the *Manitoba Free Press* to label him a "traitor"). Nonetheless, he was well-rewarded, and by the time Ross set foot in Gravely's office in May of 1884, he did so as the railroad's new land commissioner.

It was a plum appointment.

Answering directly to company president W.C. Van Horne, Ross had been tasked with assembling land for the railway's western terminus — designated as nearby Port Moody in an 1881 act of parliament. Wherever it went, the CPR enjoyed the sort of corporate influence that would make Amazon jealous; guided by the tough, uncompromising Van Horne, the company's growth had been made possible by generous land grants — Crown and private land obtained (through donation, coercion, legal trickery, or outright bullying) in exchange for the promise of future prosperity. And by the spring of 1884, there was no reason to think Port Moody would be any different. The city's designation as the terminus was enshrined in law, and in anticipation, speculators (facilitated by real estate agents like Gravely) had spent the past three years buying up every inch of available land in the region.

However, the letter in Ross's hands told a different story.

"The letter," Gravely later recalled, "was from Van Horne. I read it. It was to the effect that the terminus was to be at Coal Harbour, not Port Moody."

It's impossible to say if Gravely was Ross's first stop when he arrived on the shores of Burrard Inlet, but what's certain is that the thirty-four-year-old had access to two things Ross needed: money and contacts. With a head of fiery red hair, a drooping moustache, and a love of sailing, the Ontario native had put his Winnipeg experience to good use in the interim, buying and flipping lots in Victoria (alongside two partners, F.C. Innes and E.V. Bodwell), finally opening a real estate firm in the tiny logging community then known as Granville. In an aborted attempt at his memoirs, Gravely framed his journey west rather innocently, stating that he left Winnipeg with "the intention (in 1883) of seeing where the railway ended." This was something of an understatement. As both Ross and Gravely knew, where the CPR went, land values skyrocketed. Anyone buying up land near the western terminus — projected to be the most profitable venture along the entire rail line — stood to reap huge profits. And the man tasked with acquiring that land could tell them exactly where to buy. It would be like Winnipeg all over again — only this time, the returns would be exponentially larger.

It was the investment opportunity of a lifetime.

All they needed now were some partners.

2.

THE SYNDICATE

"Better chances for investment were never offered. Lots that can now be bought for a few hundred dollars will beyond a doubt be worth as many thousands within a year or two. Investment of only a few hundred dollars will yet return fortunes to those that have the foresight to realize the future in store for this place."

— Advertisement in *The Portland West Shore*, September 1884

ON MAY 16 OF 1885, the *Port Moody Gazette* ran the following item on its front page:

"The Coal Harbour Land Syndicate," the headline read.

Then below: "As considerable interest attaches to the above firm on account of the grievous harm that has resulted from it, not alone to Port Moody, but, we think we may truly say, to the province at large, we have taken pains to secure the names of the original stock holders. If there are any mistakes in the names or the number of shares originally held by the gentlemen respectively, we are open to correction."

The paper went on to list more than a dozen names, including "Oppenheimer Bros," "Dr. Powell," and "Messrs. Hugh and Geo. Keefer," alongside their share holdings.

"Who was in the Syndicate?" Walter Gravely later recalled. "There were A.W. Ross, who formed the Syndicate, Dr. Israel Wood Powell, Major Dupont, David Oppenheimer, Gideon Robertson and myself. Streets are named after most of them. The Syndicate bought the land from Peter Curran Dunlevy, owner of much property in D.L. 184, and to get our deeds we divided up."

Several names were conspicuously absent from the *Gazette*'s list — chief among them, Gravely and Arthur Wellington Ross. The omission of Gravely is unusual, considering his records show that he had been purchasing land in Coal Harbour with other syndicate partners since at least the spring of 1884. As for Ross, the reason was almost certainly money; by that point, after being dragged into court more than once for defrauding investors, his finances had deteriorated to the point where he was unable to afford land of his own, and instead accepted a one-fifth share in the collective as a reward for arranging the sale.

"A.W. Ross had no money," Gravely noted, "and when it came to making the first payment, he had to apply to others."

Of the shareholders, only Gravely and Oppenheimer were locals. The rest, including the Keefer brothers, Major Dupont, and Dr. Israel Wood Powell, hailed from Victoria, and virtually all of them were connected in some way with the CPR, the government, or the Winnipeg boom; George Keefer had been a railway surveyor, helping to build the route between Lytton and Boston Bar. Dr. Powell was the provincial Indian affairs superintendent. Gideon Robertson had been a major player in Winnipeg during the early

1880s — one of the many speculators (like Gravely and Ross) who had fuelled the city's housing bubble, and then walked away when it burst. He was a personal friend of Gravely's, and had made several other powerful allies including then-Provincial Secretary John Robson (who would soon invest in Coal Harbour himself). By now, rumours had been swirling for more than a year that a small group of wealthy, out-of-town investors was buying up much of the land around Coal Harbour, anticipating a change in location for the western terminus, and the rivalry between speculators in Port Moody and Coal Harbour had grown increasingly bitter. By September of 1885, the *Port Moody Gazette* was calling the gambit "an abortion, which must die in order to rid the world of something that tempts men to misfortune."

Portrait of Walter Gravely, circa 1880s.
Image Courtesy of CVA (Walter Gravely File)

"It has always been a puzzle to us how the promoters of the Coal Harbour scheme ever deceived themselves or anybody else," the paper continued, under the headline "The Fate of Sisyphus." "We are not now assuming the role of a rival storekeeper by decrying Coal Harbour and English Bay; to do so would be the height of cruelty; they have both been condemned by public opinion and are therefore beyond criticism; but we repeat the glaring objections to their adoption as the terminus of the Canadian Pacific Railway, in order to ask how anyone could be imposed upon by such a pretext."

So confident were the Port Moody speculators that they had even hosted a lavish party back in the summer of 1884, to celebrate a visit by W.C. Van Horne, Premier William Smithe, and Land Commissioner Arthur Wellington Ross. The delegation was given a hero's welcome. After being shown around the Elgin Hotel, which had been festooned with two large banners — one reading "C.P.R.W.T. (Canadian Pacific Railway, Western Terminus)" and another that read "Welcome Van Horne" — the CPR president gave a speech to the cheering crowd, detailing the financial windfall that was soon to descend on the railroad's terminal city.

"He is evidently a man of large information and mature judgement," the *Gazette* drooled, "quick to observe the natural advantage of different sections of the country, and a firm believer in the great future of British Columbia. It is his opinion that a city of 100,000 inhabitants will exist at the western terminus of the C.P.R in a few years, and though he made no direct reference as to the exact location of that future city, yet it was not hard to infer that Port Moody was in his mind's eye at the moment."

Van Horne's poker face was admirable. As the Port Moody speculators would soon discover, the debate over the western terminus had already been settled months earlier, during secret negotiations with the provincial government — and not in their favour. The official reason later given had to do with Port Moody's harbour; Van

Horne had an engineering report hastily drawn up in late 1884, citing a number of potential problems with the site.

The real reason was speculation.

"There are more speculators about New Westminster and Victoria than there were in Winnipeg during the boom and they are a much sharper lot," Van Horne wrote to CPR surveyor A.B. Rogers in December of 1884. "Nearly every person is more or less interested and you will have to be on your guard against all of them."

It isn't that Van Horne had a problem with speculation; he just wanted to make sure that the CPR, its executives, and its allies were the ones reaping the benefits. By this point, Port Moody's property values had become much higher than the railroad was willing to pay. Lots which were almost valueless a few years earlier, were now being bought and sold for anywhere from eight to fifteen hundred dollars each — transactions facilitated by real estate insiders like Walter Gravely ("I sold hundreds of lots in Port Moody," he later said, smugly, "but never once did I buy one myself"). The railroad needed a different strategy, and a broad swathe of available, inexpensive land — land that would not only serve the company's interests, but expand the personal real estate portfolios of its executives and their friends — often at the expense of locals.

One such local was John Clarke.

A marine engineer by trade, Clarke was almost certainly part of the delegation waiting on the platform to welcome Ross, Smithe, and Van Horne that summer in 1884. Like many others, he was eager to reap the benefits of the coming property boom, and by 1882, he had purchased a total of eighteen lots in Port Moody. While clearing, subdividing, and marketing the properties to investors in New Westminster and Victoria, he became active in civic development, serving as a school board trustee, chairing an incorporation committee, and helping secure lands for a harbour. He also worked tirelessly as an advocate for Port Moody landowners; in the spring of 1882, he had helped send a delegate to Ottawa to represent their interests. And a telegram Clarke received, in March, brimmed with confidence. "Everything correct," it read. "Good news by letter. Property valuable. Highest Authority."

Unfortunately for Clarke — and many like him — the CPR already had other plans; a month before Clarke received his telegram, retiring General Manager James Hill had written, in a private letter: "from all I can learn, Coal Harbour is rather more likely to become the Pacific Terminus than Port Moody." While negotiations with the provincial government began in earnest during the fall of 1884, the issue had essentially been decided six months earlier; around the same time that Gravely received his fateful visit from Arthur Wellington Ross, and acting on information provided by Van Horne, Premier William Smithe (who also happened to be chief commissioner of lands) and his good friend/Provincial Secretary John Robson began quietly purchasing land of their own near Coal Harbour. Other government representatives made similar purchases around this time: Dr. Israel Wood Powell, Superintendent of Indian Affairs, bought enough land that he remained one of the region's largest landowners until his death in 1915. Dominion Postmaster Jonathan Miller's holdings were so large, they were said to rival that of the Oppenheimers. Van Horne had few qualms about greasing the palms of government officials for his own benefit (in later correspondence with Superintendent Harry Abbott, he emphasized the importance of the Premier's cooperation, ordering Abbott to "do anything we can in his private interest" — including selling him lots at a discount), and the approach paid off; by February of 1885, only a few months after the delegation stopped at Port Moody, the CPR had been granted six thousand acres of land, including all of District Lots 526 (the south shore of False Creek/Mount Pleasant) and 541 (the modern downtown core), as well as every third lot in D.L. 181 (Strathcona), 185 (the West End), and 196 (the north shore of False

Creek/Yaletown/Gastown) — to say nothing of the substantial personal holdings of its executives and allies.

Before 1884, the land on the shores of Burrard Inlet wasn't considered much of an investment. In fact, when English settlers John Morton, Samuel Brighouse, and William Hailstone decided to acquire 550 acres of District Lot 185, they were ridiculed for their naivete.

"Father told me that when some of the New Westminster people heard that they had agreed to purchase or preempt the land at one dollar per acre, payable to the government, that the three of them were dubbed the 'three greenhorn Englishmen'," Morton's son Joseph later recalled, "and some people enjoyed a great laugh at their expense."

At the time, that laughter seemed justified. From a European perspective, District Lot 185 was essentially in the middle of nowhere. New Westminster — then the provincial capital — was considered the seat of power and culture in the region (such as it was), and by 1873, the shores of Burrard Inlet were home to just sixty-five settlers, split between two small townsites — Hastings and Granville (known colloquially as "Gastown," after flamboyant saloon-owner John "Gassy Jack" Deighton). Back in the 1860s, the surrounding land had been divided into vast, numbered district lots by Colonel Richard Moody and his Royal Engineers (who became the region's first speculators, snapping up plenty of property for themselves and flipping it at a profit). Despite the lots being offered at rock-bottom prices (in an effort to entice new settlers, the process of pre-emption allowed them to purchase land for roughly one dollar per acre), they were widely seen as valueless; there were few roads, few amenities, and few employment prospects outside of Edward Stamp's saw mill, largely a stopping point for transient labourers.

"Prior to 1885, Granville was nothing more than a secluded pioneer settlement," early Vancouverite W.H. Gallagher later noted. "[A] clearing, three hundred and fifty yards along the shore, two hundred and fifty yards into the forest, boxed in by tall trees; damp, wet, the actual clearing littered with stumps and forest debris, and a pro-fusion of undergrowth, including luxuriant skunk cabbage."

District Lot 185 was particularly remote, only accessible by fum-bling along twelve miles of overgrown trails; the area was lush with greenery — swampland, and, according to Joseph Morton, old growth forest "so prolific over that country that the tops shut out the light." The forests teemed with elk, beaver, bears, and cougars, and their only neighbours were members of the Squamish, Musqueam, and Tsleil-waututh nations who had occupied the surrounding region for more than four thousand years. And at the time, there's no indication the trio saw much of a future in their acquisition; Morton, who came from a family of potters, thought Coal Harbour's clay deposits might make it an ideal site for brick-making (it wasn't). Brighouse and Hailstone wanted grazing land for their cows.

"[T]hey had no idea there would ever be a Vancouver," Gallagher added. "Brighouse himself told me what they wanted the land for. He preempted it because he did not want others bothering him. He also told me that when the man who was surveying it was laying out the boundaries, the man said to him, 'I will put in the island (Dead-man's Island) in your preemption for five dollars.' Hailstone, so Brighouse told me, said, 'Don't give it him; we've enough stuff now.'"

In any event, the three men sent a poorly-written letter of con-sideration to the government in November of 1862, asking for approximately 150 acres each in District Lot 185, and in short order Morton had cleared a half-acre, and built a cabin on the bluff near what is now the one thousand block of Hastings Street. Legally, pre-emption required that the buyer reside on the property, and on paper, the trio had claimed to be taking turns sharing the cabin. In reality, the task fell to Morton. Luckily, he was a hardy sort; in addi-tion to working as a cattle rancher in the Thompson Valley, he had done two stints as a Cariboo miner — during which he had walked the four-hundred-mile trail to and from the region twice. And while his first months were somewhat tense, he quickly became acquainted with the region and its residents.

"Mr. Morton stayed in the cabin, and sometimes slept in the woods; he was afraid of the Indians," Morton's wife Ruth later explained. "But he stayed there so long that, by and by, he learned to speak Chinook, and finally got very friendly with the Indians. His sisters used to send out to him from Yorkshire — 'to The Three Pioneers' they were sent — some little skull caps made of coloured cloth, like the English public school boys wear to designate the school colours — and the Indians always like lots of colour, and the Indians were very well pleased when Mr. Morton gave them the coloured caps."

Over the ensuing decade, the land in District Lot 185 didn't appreciate markedly in value, and by 1881 — confirming the worst predictions of the naysayers in New Westminster — the Three Greenhorns were in financial trouble. Unable to keep up with taxes, they found themselves at risk of losing their property altogether — and they very well might have, if it weren't for the appearance of an unlikely saviour: a soft-spoken German-Jewish immigrant named David Oppenheimer. Then in his late forties, Oppenheimer had a solid track record as a businessman, and a knack for making money. Alongside his brothers Charles and Isaac, he had amassed a fortune in resource communities across BC, both in the wholesale grocery business, and in the buying and selling of real estate. Like Arthur Wellington Ross and Walter Gravely, Oppenheimer had CPR connections, having worked as an engineer through the Rocky Mountains, and like Ross and Gravely, he had an intimate understanding of the CPR's effect on property values. Two years before the arrival of W.C. Van Horne's fateful letter, Oppenheimer saw the potential of the land surrounding Coal Harbour — an insight that would lead him to become a major player in civic growth over the next decade.

His timing couldn't have been more perfect.

By this point, Hailstone had had enough; rather than pay the outstanding taxes, he sold his share for a pittance (said to have been a twenty-dollar gold piece, several sacks of flour, and a feral horse) and returned to England. Suddenly, Morton and Brighouse found themselves with a new business partner. Working alongside Oppenheimer, they plotted a new strategy, clearing and subdividing portions of D.L. 185 into lots for individual sale, and even began marketing it as the "City of Liverpool."

The endeavour ultimately went nowhere.

"Land! Who wanted land?" scoffed pioneer John Scales. "There was lots of land; land wasn't worth anything. My sons say to me sometimes, 'Why didn't you buy land? See how well off you'd have been now.' I know all about the mistakes I've made, but land; why there was lots of land."

Scales wasn't alone in his assessment. In 1883, developer James Weldon Horne — who had made a fortune in real estate and construction back in Winnipeg — surveyed the area, and decided it was too early to make any purchases. In one instance, a man in Victoria traded a Vancouver lot for a bottle of rum. Despite the best efforts of Oppenheimer and the two remaining Greenhorns, locals and speculators had virtually no interest in investing in the region.

That was all about to change.

"Mayor Oppenheimer had a lot of land in the east, and the west too," city pioneer H.P. McCraney later noted. "Those who were in the know bought all they could lay their hands on. They knew the railroad was coming, and simply got it first."

According to Gravely's records, he had begun making purchases almost immediately after reading Van Horne's letter in the spring of 1884, and he and various other syndicate members continued their buying spree well into the following year. Disregarding Ross' caution to "tell no one" of the letter's contents, Gravely even took out an ad in the Portland-based *West Shore*, in September of 1884, geared specifically toward American speculators.

"Better chances for investment were never offered," it read. "Lots that can now be bought for a few hundred dollars will beyond a doubt be worth as many thousands within a year or two."

During this period, Oppenheimer in particular was working double-duty, advancing the railroad's interests while simultaneously padding his own pocketbook. While Lots 526 and 541 were directly granted to the railway, Lots 181, 185, and 196 were privately owned. This presented a problem for the notoriously tight-fisted CPR, and it fell to men like Oppenheimer to convince those landowners to part with a portion of their holdings — something many, including John Morton, weren't particularly keen to do. Undeterred, Oppenheimer personally visited his old partner — who, by now, was living in the Fraser Valley — with the express purpose of badgering him into submission.

"He told me he did it reluctantly," Reverend P.C. Parker, a long-time friend, later recalled. "Morton said to me, 'I did not want to give them every third lot,' and then stressed that the C.P.R. had a charter from ocean to ocean, and what was the use of giving them every third lot. 'But,' Mr. Morton said, 'they bothered me and bothered me.'"

In some ways, Oppenheimer's persistence was understandable; by the fall of 1885, he had been working to secure signatures for much of the year. He was also the largest shareholder in the Coal Harbour Land Syndicate — a speculative investment that would return very little until the railway was complete and property values began to rise — and was beginning to feel financially overstretched.

"I have spent a great deal of time personally visiting the mainland several times in securing signatures to these agreements," he wrote to W.C. Van Horne in October, "having had to incur considerable expense and much anxiety. I trust with the explanations given they will be accepted by your company without delay."

During all of this, speculators in Port Moody remained blissfully unaware of the railway's machinations. On the surface, they continued to express confidence in their investment through the summer of 1885 — even after receiving word that the CPR has dispatched surveyor Lachlan Alexander Hamilton to the area near Coal Harbour.

"There appeared in last Saturday's *Columbian* as choice an assortment of cast iron lies as it has been our lot to meet in a journalistic experience of some years," fumed the *Gazette,* after reading reports of Hamilton's upcoming visit in the *New Westminster British Columbian.* "According to the paper referred to, Mr. Van Horne made some of the most extraordinary statements that ever fell from the lips of a man in his position. Now we have it on the best possible authority — from gentlemen who attended the meeting, and from Mr. Van Horne himself — that no such statements were made, nor was anything said that could be construed into such a meaning.[...] At Port Moody we have every essential and the ROAD IS ALREADY HERE. That it will remain here for all time there is not the slightest reason to doubt — the contradictory and prevaricating *Columbian* to the contrary notwithstanding."

Then, in December, Clarke and the other investors received a letter from the Governor General, admitting the unthinkable: the CPR was indeed discussing an extension to their terminus. Many didn't believe it. Others began to panic. Clarke and his contemporaries sent multiple petitions to Ottawa, begging the the railway to reconsider. When that didn't work, they filed an injunction against the CPR, and the resulting legal battle stretched on for almost eighteen months, going all the way to the Supreme Court before it was finally overturned by Judge Matthew Baillie Begbie. Property values plummeted, and in the aftermath, Port Moody investors lost their shirts. Lots purchased for eight hundred dollars during the height of the 1885 speculation boom were now going for less than two hundred. Clarke had no choice but to offload his property for next to nothing — including his own house — and returned, chastened, to his job as an engineer. Some investors tried to plead with Superintendent Harry Abbott for compensation — a request Abbott flatly denied, replying that, in essence, it was their own fault for paying fifteen hundred dollars for lots worth only fifteen.

Another big loser in the deal was Arthur Wellington Ross; in November of 1884, he had been forced to surrender his interest in the syndicate under embarrassing circumstances.

Arthur Wellington Ross and family outside his real estate office, Granville BC, circa 1886 (note the potential speculators examining lot prices written on a rock to the right of the building).
Image courtesy of CVA.

"A sheriff tapped Ross on the shoulder as soon as he touched the wharf [in Victoria]," Walter Gravely later recalled. "It was a most awkward situation for Ross; he had come up on the boat with Van Horne and here he was under arrest as soon as he landed. Some clergyman in Australia had entrusted some funds to him for which it was said he had not accounted. It was a week or so before we found out. When we did we went to a lawyer, had him draw up an assignment — I have the document yet — and conveyed to us his interest. The outcome was that Oppenheimer and Dupont got out of the trouble, but in getting out, Ross gave our property, 1,400 or 1,500 acres in what is now Grandview, as security for their advances to him personally."

But in the days after the ink had dried on the CPR land grant, Van Horne, the railroad, and the other members of the syndicate must have been very pleased indeed. In the two years that followed, the railroad would make almost $870,000 from the sale of granted land in Coal Harbour, and by 1889, the proceeds of those sales had made them more money than every other company town in Canada combined. Syndicate members, too, became exceedingly wealthy; Walter Gravely would settle in the posh West End, where he counted sugar magnate B.T. Rogers among his neighbours. He would ultimately build a real estate firm with F.C. Innes, his old partner from the Victoria days, and went on to found the Royal Vancouver Yacht Club. He lived until the age of eighty-six, his birthday — alongside a photo — being published each year in the pages of *The Vancouver Province*. Men like the Keefers and David Oppenheimer would go on to occupy even greater roles in civic life. Before a single lot had been put up for official sale, and after six months of negotiations and twelve months of backroom dealings, they had succeeded in outfoxing their rivals, and — whether personally or on behalf of the company — made the real estate investment of a lifetime.

The next step was to turn that investment into a city.

3.

INCORPORATION, INC.

*"I fancy that I can see Vancouver when her hour
has come. I see the residences of the well-to-do
crowded out of the narrow limits of the peninsula
and spreading [...] a part of the city too expensive
for ordinary folks to have houses there, not
private or select enough for the very rich except
in the remoter part facing English Bay, with its
fine, sandy beach, and its proximity to the park."*

— **Douglas Sladen**, *Frank Leslie's Popular Monthly*, **1891**

BEFORE LACHLAN Alexander Hamilton's office opened on the morning of March 6, 1886, a lineup had already begun to form.

"I was fifth or sixth in the line," Walter Gravely later recalled. "Dr. LeFevre was second; F.C. Innes was third; then came R.G. Tatlow; C.D. Rand was next, and I was behind C.D. Rand."

And in the front, his hand resting anxiously on the doorknob, stood Alfred G. Ferguson. Ferguson (owner of the Ferguson Block, where he and Hamilton both kept offices), had stayed up all night, camped out beside a wood stove in his office for the opportunity to be first in line. Every man who stood outside Hamilton's office was connected to the CPR or the Coal Harbour Land Syndicate; Ferguson was a railway contractor, and brother-in-law of prominent realtor Henry Ceperly (himself friend and future partner of Arthur Wellington Ross). Lefevre had worked as a physician for the CPR. Innes was friend and partner to Walter Gravely, and owner of the city's oldest real estate firm, opened in the spring of 1885. Tatlow knew David Oppenheimer, and would soon be selling lots directly on the Syndicate's behalf. Charles D. Rand was one of the city's most prominent realtors, as well as the Syndicate's secretary. Approximately two weeks earlier, Hamilton and Ferguson — alongside Arthur Wellington Ross — had convened an incorporation committee with the intent of drafting a petition to Victoria that would transform the sleepy logging community of Granville into a full-fledged city. The committee's existence had come at the urging of Provincial Secretary John Robson, who had made a speech to Granville's residents in early January, a speech which had been as much public address as it was CPR sales pitch.

"The Hon. Mr. Robson (whose appearance on the platform was greeted with applause), spoke for over an hour," gushed the *New Westminster British Columbian* (a paper which was owned by Robson), "and he earnestly exhorted them, in any movement of that kind, to act openly and above board, consulting, and as far as possible, acting in harmony with the Canadian Pacific Railway Company and others largely interested in the great city of the future."

Robson went on to extoll "the bright prospects opening up before the people of Granville" and warning residents "against taking any course calculated to divide the community into contending factions at this the supreme moment, when it was of such vital importance to pull together as one man."

Of course, Robson didn't mention what he personally stood to gain from incorporation; while actively deriding speculators as "soil-grabbers" in the legislature, he had been sitting on land in Coal Harbour, purchased at W.C. Van Horne's direction, for a year and a half. And a great many others in the audience would likely have also been rubbing their hands with glee — Gravely and Ferguson among them. Unsurprisingly, their names appear among the petition's signatories, alongside others like Lefevre, Innes, and Samuel Brighouse. With news of incorporation quickly picking up steam, speculators and developers were flooding into the area — including big fish such as James Weldon Horne (who had first scoped out the city back in 1883) — anxious to get their hands on as much property as they could.

They were about to get their chance.

Hamilton had recently replaced Arthur Wellington Ross as the CPR's land commissioner, and when his office doors opened at 9:00 that morning, the railroad's first public land auction would officially begin. The terms were tough: six per cent annual interest, with one-third cash up-front, one-third within six months, and the final payment due by the end of the year. That said, the CPR was willing to provide discounts of twenty to thirty per cent if buyers agreed to construct buildings valued at more than two thousand dollars.

"Why is this?" asked journalist Douglas Sladen, in an issue of *Frank Leslie's Popular Monthly*, then the most widely-read magazine of its day. "Because of the attitude of the principal land-owners, the Canadian Pacific Railroad, who, determined to avoid the prostration which followed the boom at Winnipeg, have prevented the speculative buying of land..."

Certainly the railroad still had the Winnipeg bust firmly in mind. But, as before, the issue wasn't strictly about speculation. If it had been, Van Horne and his affiliates might have kept a sharp eye on realtors like Ross, Gravely, and Gideon Robertson, who had been largely responsible for the collapse of the Winnipeg market back in 1881.

These punishing terms were actually designed to crowd out all but the wealthiest speculators — in this case, the CPR and its allies. When it came to real estate, the railroad was far and away the biggest game in town; thanks to the generous grant from Premier William Smithe, they owned an estimated eight times more than their closest competitor — the Coal Harbour Syndicate — and their chief concern was for those land values to rise. For this to happen, the population would have to rise well beyond where it stood, then at a paltry four hundred. Neighbourhoods would need to be cleared, roads built, a downtown core established. But the first order of business — at least for Van Horne — was that Granville needed a rebranding.

"The facts are, we talked about the name 'Vancouver' under the Maple Tree," early resident (and undertaker) Frank Hart later recalled. "We talked a lot about it; they said it was confusing on account of Vancouver's Island [sic], but we made no decision. How could we make a decision? We had no voice in the matter. [...] We all knew that Van Horne was the actual power who would decide what the name would be."

The idea of the name change seems to have first surfaced in the summer of 1884, in a letter between Van Horne and surveyor L.A. Hamilton, but despite the CPR president's government influence, it wasn't initially well received by locals.

"The feeling was so bitter that we kept the name both in our letterheads and other stationery and directed all our correspondence to Granville just the same," Hart continued. "The thing was so annoying to the postmaster and the powers-that-were that he got orders from somewhere to himself and the police to go around town and notify each and everyone, the storekeepers especially, to change our names on the first of May."

Van Horne's choice was also met with little enthusiasm in the legislature, with Kootenay representative R.L. Galbraith complaining: "The selection of the present name was not a matter of local option at all, but was forced on the citizens of that place by an agent of the c.p.r."

Nonetheless, Van Horne was undeterred. "All through he stuck firmly to the name," L.A. Hamilton later wrote, "even when parliament at Victoria discussed the inadvisability of calling the terminus by that name, and showed their opposition to it."

In Feb of 1886, shortly before the land auction, Vancouver had one hundred buildings. By May, roughly a month after the city was officially incorporated, it was up to six hundred. There was just one problem: the newly-christened city needed a government. *An Act Incorporating the City of Vancouver* had been passed in early April, which meant that an election was imminent, and the real estate industry (in this case, the Coal Harbour Syndicate and the CPR) needed aldermen who could represent their interests. They needed a council with a development agenda. And most importantly, they needed a mayor they could trust.

Luckily, they had just the man for the job.

Malcolm Alexander McLean was a robust Scotsman with a kindly disposition and a head of prematurely white hair, known affectionately amongst his friends as "Squire." In addition to being a real estate agent and land speculator during the Winnipeg bust, MacLean was also Arthur Wellington Ross's brother-in-law. The pair had moved to Winnipeg together in 1878, where both men gained — and lost — a fortune during the market crash. When MacLean arrived in Vancouver in January of 1886, it was as a guest of Ross' wife, and as the interim proprietor of Ross' real estate business (Ross was in Ottawa at the time). Immediately after his arrival, he went about purchasing a house and two stores, and by May of 1886, had left his partnership with Ross and started a real estate firm of his own. At the time of the election, MacLean had no experience in politics, and no interest in running for office. The only other contender for mayor was one Richard Alexander, head of the nearby

Hastings Mill. Alexander too had been part of the incorporation committee, and understood the value of development, but his interests were seen to be more closely identified with the fate of the resource industry than the consortium of railroad and real estate interests intent on determining the growth of the city. He was also wildly unpopular. As the head of the city's largest employer, he had made few friends amongst the loggers who made up much of Granville's population.

"Well, as they were going to run Richard Alexander for mayor, I thought we ought to have someone to oppose him," said pioneer (an early policeman) Jackson Abray, "the arrangements had all been made for him to run for mayor. So I saw Angus Fraser, and Simon, his brother; both these men were loggers, and the loggers did not have much use for Alexander; very little use [...] The three of us went around to Abbott Street where MacLean had a little real estate office, and interviewed him. I made him acquainted with the two Frasers and they shook hands, and I asked him if he would run for mayor."

"MacLean said, 'Why, I have no dollars for an election.'"

"I replied, 'We have a few dollars; if you'll make up your mind to come out.'"

The campaign that followed was rife with dirty tricks.

Both candidates were happy to bend the rules when it suited them (for example, Alexander brought in a boatload of Chinese-Canadians from Victoria in hopes of having them vote), but MacLean's team resorted to outright fraud; technically, the franchise was only extended to property owners (particularly white, male ones), so the MacLean camp began simply writing multiple names onto the same lease.

"Mr. Alexander was defeated, but not fairly," recalled early resident W.H. Gallagher. "One man had a lease to a portion of a building on Cordova Street, and came down to vote with the lease in his hand and voted on it. Mr. MacLean's committee persuaded him to leave the lease with them; it was drawn up in the usual form with a space for the name, and I think fifty men must have voted on that lease. After one man had voted, the next voter's name was written on a slip of paper and pasted in the space on the lease where the name appeared, and so continued until there was a tier of slips, and they were removed, and a fresh start was made."

"We wanted to put MacLean in, and we did it," explained resident V.W. Haywood. "I had a vote because I rented a piece of ground on what is now Cordova Street from Arthur Sullivan, built a cabin on it, and voted on that cabin as a tenant. There was a lot of people who voted who did not have a vote. Lots of people coming in here, stopping in hotels; they had no qualification, but, as I said, we wanted to put in MacLean, and we did."

At the end of a hard-fought day, the MacLean camp stood victorious by only seventeen votes. And from that moment onward, the interests of City Hall and the interests of the real estate industry became virtually impossible to distinguish. Between 1886 and 1894, nine of Vancouver's fourteen largest property owners sat on city council. During roughly the same period, three of the city's six mayors were extensively involved in real estate. On the first council, three men represented both real estate and the railroad; MacLean, alongside newly-minted aldermen L.A. Hamilton and Robert Balfour (who had served as the CPR's superintendent of bridge construction). In relatively short order, one more (Harry Hemlow) would go on to work for the BC Electric Railway Company, a consortium funded by real estate interests to open up new city areas for development.

By June of 1886, Vancouver's six hundred buildings had grown to eight hundred. By the end of the year, a total of $1.5 million would be spent on construction. Ultimately, the CPR would net more from the sale of land in Vancouver than in every other company town in the country, combined. Incorporation also proved to be a windfall for CPR insiders, and for the Syndicate; by 1887, David Oppenheimer's initial investment — $52,000 if the estimates in the *Gazette* are to be believed — had grown to at least $125,000. Dr. Israel Wood Powell's shares had increased by twenty-five thousand. W.C. Van Horne would go on to own the largest commercial building on Granville Street. John Robson, who had spent so much time speaking out against other speculators, also made a killing on his Coal Harbour property; by 1892, he was described in a letter as "the most successful land speculator in the province," with holdings in excess of five hundred thousand. Even John Morton, who had been forced to give up one-third of his land, died with an estate valued at roughly seven hundred thousand.

Malcolm MacLean went on to serve two terms in the Mayor's chair; the key promise of his second campaign was to restrict the property rights of Vancouver's ethnic Chinese residents. In 1893, he was given a plum position with the Dominion Government, as the special commissioner of immigration in the US. His job was, what would later be dubbed by the industry "place marketing", writing articles and lecturing on the benefits of moving to the west coast. While he didn't get rich, Arthur Wellington Ross opened a real estate firm with Henry Ceperly, and the pair remained involved in Vancouver's place marketing campaigns into the early 1890s. As an MP, Ross feared he had worn out his welcome, but the CPR — looking to reward him for his hard work in BC — pulled out all the stops during his 1887 campaign, paying to have Ross voters sent by train to nearby polling stations. For the next ten years, Ross was a relative nonentity in the House of Commons, however, he never lost his thirst for a quick buck; in 1901, while investigating a speculative timber venture in the BC interior, he suffered a stroke, and died in hospital two days before his fifty-fifth birthday.

Shortly after the CPR land auction opened to the public, the city's prominent real estate people began an aggressive place marketing campaign of their own, one that continued well into the early 1890s.

Vancouver was suddenly the "Constantinople of the West," and an "astonishing field for investment." The CPR became the "magician that has transformed British Columbia." When an advertorial in *Frank Leslie's Popular Monthly* required lot prices, they were provided by the firm of Ross & Ceperly. Statistics on commerce were furnished by the Oppenheimer Brothers. The Syndicate soon rebranded itself as the "Vancouver Land and Improvement Company," (the Vancouver Improvement Company, or VIC for short), and in partnership with agents like R.G. Tatlow, began selling their subdivided lots for $350 each.

And while he wasn't the first in line, standing outside Hamilton's office on that March morning in 1886, it's likely that Walter Gravely would have allowed himself a private smile.

"There was no rush," he later gloated.

After all, he had quietly purchased his first lot months before the auction had even begun. The boom was officially underway. By 1887, Vancouver would have twelve grocery stores and sixteen real estate firms.

However, while the glee felt by Gravely and the Syndicate would continue, the CPR's wouldn't last. No sooner had they secured their investment, then it had come under attack.

4.

THE PARK

"Say Liz, if you take my advice you'll buy a lot on the North Shore opposite Hastings Park right this afternoon, before you go home."

"Oh I don't think I'm especially interested in real estate, and Dad wouldn't like me to." Lizzie Laidlaw placidly set her white teeth into another piece of cake.

"Well, it's a sure thing this time anyway," said Mrs. Morely, decisively, "and when everyone else is making fortunes, Lizzie Laidlaw will have herself to thank if she gets left out."

"If so many people are making fortunes, Rose," replied Lizzie gently, "someone must be losing them. I'd just hate to make a pile of money out of someone else's loss."

— Hilda Glynn-Ward, "The Writing On The Wall," 1921

AUGUST JACK KHATSALANO and his sister Louise were sitting down to breakfast one morning in the summer of 1887 when they heard a noise from outside.

"Somebody hit the outside of the house," he later recalled, "and my sister Louise—she is older than I was—and I ran out and said to a whiteman, 'What are you doing?'"

The "whiteman" was a government surveyor, and what he was doing was cutting the corner off of their house.

"The whiteman said he was going to build a road," Khatsahlano continued. "There were two of them; they were surveying, and they had a surveying rod with them. They cut off the corner of our house, just a little bit, so that they could see where to put their survey line [...] The man said that 'when the road goes by here you are going to have lots of money.'"

August Jack — then around ten years old — and his sister lived in a settlement known as Chaythoos, one of several Coast Salish villages scattered throughout the one thousand acre, forested area north of District Lot 185 (the modern-day West End). While they were the third generation of the Khatsahlano family to live in the area, it had been home to First Nations communities for millennia; a complex interweaving of various Coast Salish peoples, including Squamish, Musqueam, and Tsleil-Watuth. Archaeological examination of numerous found objects in the region — including human remains from a large midden excavated nearby — demonstrate human activity in the area going back at least three thousand years.

"Untold ages past men lived on this clearing," City Archivist J.S. Matthews later wrote. "In 1792, when Captain Vancouver sailed by, Squamish lived here in huge cedar slab houses, one slope roofs, built with stone hammers and chisels."

The most prominent settlement in the area was called X̱wáy̓x̱way (pronounced "Whoi Whoi"). Stretching across the northern end of the peninsula, it had been named for the masked dance Potlatch ceremonies that regularly took place there, and was home to at least a dozen buildings — including a two-hundred-foot by sixty-foot "Big House" where the ceremonies were held (when Dominion Postmaster Jonathan Miller witnessed one such ceremony in the pre-incorporation days, he estimated it was attended by ten thousand people). While historians believe that BC's pre-contact population numbered more than twenty thousand, the European introduction of smallpox devastated Indigenous communities — X̱wáýx̱way in particular — to the point that, by the time of August Jack's birth, the village was home to only one hundred people.

"A dreadful skin disease, loathsome to look upon, broke out upon all alike," a Squamish Nation resident told cultural anthropologist Charles Hill-Tout near the turn of the century. "None were spared. Men, women, and children sickened, took the disease and died in agony by the hundreds, so that when the spring arrived and fresh food was procurable, there was scarcely a person left of all their numbers to get it."

Nonetheless, X̱wáýx̱way remained a popular site for Potlatch ceremonies until at least 1885. Within the hierarchy of the Coast Salish, the Khatsahlano family was about as high-ranking as they came, with a home at Chaythoos, and another in the nearby village of Snauq (near the modern-day foot of the Burrard Street Bridge). Their father, the chief of the Squamish Nation (called "Supplejack" by Europeans), had died shortly after August Jack was born, and was buried above ground in a wooden mausoleum on the X̱wáýx̱way property. Unlike many other families, they owned cows and a pair of horses. The residents of Chaythoos and X̱wáýx̱way had coexisted in relative harmony with one another, and with European settlers for the forty plus years leading up to incorporation. Europeans had dispensed rifles to members of the Squamish Nation, with the understanding that First Nations and European settlers would defend opposite sides of the downtown peninsula in the event of an

American attack. Some had even intermarried, and by the 1880s, the area near X̱wáýx̱way was surprisingly cosmopolitan, and was home to several mixed-race families, including that of Joseph "Portugese Joe" Silvey (who had married into the Khatsahalano family), and a Chinese-Canadian settlement near modern-day Anderson Point.

But not for much longer.

During the initial government survey in 1858, 788 Acres in Point Grey, 110 surrounding Jerry's Cove (named for logger Jerry Rogers, and later rechristened "Jericho"), and 155 acres on English Bay were designated as reserve land for the British navy. At the time, fear of American annexation was at the forefront of Governor James Douglas's mind, and Moody capitalized on that fear to set aside an additional one thousand acres at the north end of the future downtown peninsula, citing the cliffs of Prospect Point as being of strategic importance. In reality, Moody's motivations were money and real estate; during the initial survey of Coal Harbour, he and his secretary Robert Burnaby recognized its potential — both due to ample evidence of coal deposits, and as a speculative investment (later historical accounts describe Moody's actions as "land-grabbing").

"If ever the great railroad comes near this way, we shall be in possession of the most commanding position in the country!" Burnaby wrote, in a letter to his brother.

Despite the military designation, the land was never utilized by the British Admiralty, and in 1884, it was conveyed to the Canadian government. When making his initial demands for a provincial land grant in 1885, W.C. Van Horne had requested a sizeable portion of the military reserve, in hopes of using it as a right of way to English Bay — then the preferred site for the company's western terminus. He wrote to L.A. Hamilton, instructing him to "determine how much of the ground should be retained by the Government for defensive purposes, and how much they can spare to us." Unfortunately, while Premier Smithe's palms had been primed for greasing, Ottawa was less enthusiastic about parting with the land. It was the only time during the acquisition process that the CPR was seriously rebuffed. Then, in January of 1886, the provincial government auctioned off portions of another former military reserve on the south shore of English Bay (land the CPR had been working to obtain), and this no doubt spooked railroad executives, who began to worry about the effect on its own property values if one thousand acres of prime downtown real estate were suddenly to be made available for purchase. Suddenly, it was essential to find a way to boost the value of the railroad's holdings, while simultaneously keeping the land off the market.

It didn't take long before they came up with a plan.

Throughout the mid-1800s, an anti-modernist movement had sprung up across North America, largely in response to the crowding, pollution, and poor sanitation in most major cities. Inspired by the work of Frederick Law Olmstead and Calvert Vaux — who had been responsible for the creation of Central Park in the 1850s — urban parks began to appear in a number of North American cities, and as the CPR well knew, their effect on property values had been significant. Central Park was essentially an elite creation, championed by speculators to boost the value of their uptown properties. The same had been true in the Assiniboine Park area of Winnipeg — adopted hometown of Arthur Wellington Ross. After the CPR's plans to acquire the reserve failed, it was Ross who first petitioned the federal government, requesting the transfer of lands for a public park. This too proved a failure. Luckily, Ross still had plenty of powerful friends — at all levels of government.

"[T]he great credit for securing [Stanley Park] as a park has always been given to Mayor Oppenheimer," wrote then-Alderman L.A. Hamilton. "If the records were available it would show that the chief credit should be given to A.W. Ross and Alderman Hamilton. We both worked together to attain this object, the former as an M.P. using his influence with the Dominion Government, and the latter with the Canadian Pacific Railway by getting the chief officials at Montréal to use their influence with the government of the day."

Bear cubs chained up outside James Quiney Real Estate, circa 1910. Image courtesy of CVA.

After taking W.C. Van Horne on a scenic boat ride of the prospective park, Ross brought the idea to Hamilton and his brother-in-law Malcolm MacLean, and at Ross' urging, MacLean drafted a petition to Victoria, requesting that "the said reserve should be handed over to the [City of Vancouver]." This time, the strategy worked, and in June of 1887, the province leased the land to the city for parkland (though for the better part of a year, it would be known simply as "The Park"). It was a home run for the city's real estate interests. Unfortunately, it meant something very different to those who lived there. Between 1887 and 1889, virtually every one of the remaining families — including the Khatsahalanos — were unceremoniously evicted. Their homes were destroyed, their livestock slaughtered, and their property confiscated. The midden near X̱wáy̓x̱way — containing centuries of Coast Salish remains — was excavated, and its contents used to pave the new Park Drive. Even the remains of August Jack's father were removed. In January of 1889, city Health Inspector A.M. Robertson recommended the destruction of all remaining First Nations homes in the park, citing concerns about smallpox. A small handful managed to resist the evictions, but most — including the Chinese Canadians at Anderson Point — received harsh treatment at the hands of police and park officials.

"The Park Board ordered the Chinamen to leave the park," explained Sarah Avison, daughter of then-Park Ranger Henry Avison, "but the Chinamen would not go, so the Park Board told my father to set fire to the buildings [. . .] What happened to the Chinese I do not know, but the pigs were set loose and the bull untied, and they got lost in the forest of Stanley Park, and they could not track them down until the snow fell. Then my Dad tracked them down, and they shot them in the bushes, and the bull's head was cut off, and my father had it stuffed and set up in our hallway in our house, the 'Park Cottage.'"

The park was officially opened on September 27 of 1888, to considerable civic fanfare, at a ceremony held — to add insult to injury — on the former site of Supplejack's grave at Prospect Point. Beaming from the audience were dignitaries from the upper echelons of government and industry, including John Robson, CPR Superintendent Harry Abbott, and Vancouver's recently-elected second mayor: David Oppenheimer.

"Art will unite with nature in making this the finest park on the continent," Oppenheimer declared, speaking through this thick German accent from a raised platform in front of the Khatsalano home, "a place of recreation in the vicinity of a city where its inhabitants can spend some time amid the beauties of nature away from the busy haunts of men."

In another cruel twist for the evicted families, the newly-appointed park board was made up largely of real estate professionals, including R.G. Tatlow and A.G. Ferguson. The remaining inhabitants — eight families in total — fought back through legal channels, making an argument for adverse possession that continued into the 1920s. Skeptical of First Nations testimony, and fearful of setting a precedent for Aboriginal land title, the Supreme Court ultimately overturned their case. The only residents allowed to remain were Tim and Agnes Cummings, who lived in a small cottage near modern-day Brockton Point until 1958, paying five dollars per month in rent. Upon Tim Cummings' death, and against the pleas of heritage advocates, the cottage was demolished at the direction of a young alderman named George Puil.

While the park was a financial windfall for the railroad and the Vancouver Improvement Company, only one resident of the Stanley Park peninsula ever received money for their displacement, and it only came after her death: an elderly Squamish Nation woman called "Aunt Sally," who died days before her eviction in 1923, and whose daughter later received an out-of-court settlement with the city. The Stanley Park families were among the first victims of Vancouver's wealthy business elite, and its boundless real estate ambition.

They wouldn't be the last.

"They said, 'Pay to go through your place,'" August Jack recalled, roughly fifty years later. "But they have not paid yet."

5.

"THOSE WHO OWN THE EARTH"

"I am convinced there is a scheme on foot by a certain class in the city to make these lands their exclusive reserve by inducing the Government to have them placed on the market in such a way as to bar out the Working Class. 1) By having the land sold by auction for spot cash, 2) by compelling purchaser to build an expensive home on his property, and 3) by doing a lot of improvements in the neighbourhood to run the price of land beyond the reach of the average working man."

— *The Vancouver Province*, August 6, 1906

AT THE END OF 1889, the *Vancouver Daily World* devoted a portion of its front page to a list of the city's biggest taxpayers.

"Those who own the Earth," the headline read, "and Supply Grease for the Wheel Accordingly."

This was barely hyperbole; as the paper revealed, eighty-five per cent of property in Vancouver was owned by just 130 people. Of that total, fifty per cent was owned by only twenty people, with the remaining fifteen per cent divided amongst roughly ten thousand inhabitants.

"Our Real Estate Is Well Distributed," *The World* concluded. "Only a Few Very Heavy Owners."

Of the "Heavy Owners" who dominated the list, a number of familiar names emerge, including J.W. Horne (assessed at $3.4 million in today's dollars), A.G. Ferguson ($3.5 million), and the Vancouver Improvement Company ($7 million). Also sitting in the top five was David Oppenheimer. By the end of 1889, the soft-spoken Oppenheimer was arguably the most powerful man in Vancouver. Not only did he and his brothers hold roughly $4.2 million in assets (in addition to his VIC shares, making him the single largest private landowner in the city), he also headed the Vancouver Board of Trade and, in 1888, had succeeded Malcolm MacLean as Mayor. Aided by a staunchly pro-development council (including newly-elected alderman/speculator J.W. Horne), Oppenheimer helped spearhead a speculation and housing boom that would continue through the early 1890s. The prevailing conditions were certainly favourable. Following the arrival of the first coast-to-coast CPR passenger train, Vancouver had entered a period of rapid growth, its population doubling in size each year between 1886 and 1890. During the same period, property values also rose swiftly; in 1886, a lot near Granville and Dunsmuir was selling for four hundred dollars. By 1893, a lot in the same area sold for $1,100.

But not all the benefits were shared equally.

Thanks to Oppenheimer, the CPR, and a compliant council, a small handful of wealthy real estate oligarchs essentially ran the city, and employed whatever tactics they could to consolidate their power. During this period, the real estate industry was given carte blanche; speculation, Oppenheimer argued, was to be courted, and any attempt to float legislation taxing speculative investment or license real estate brokers was summarily ignored. As evidence, when CPR lands in Fairview went on sale in 1890, 210 of the 371 lots sold were purchased by only nine buyers. And throughout the 1890s to 1900s, a staggering forty per cent of lot owners in nearby District Lot 301 were absentee. The industry also tried a brief (and abortive) attempt at self-regulation — although this too was little more than a power grab. Formed in March of 1888, the Vancouver Real Estate Board was a fifty-member body whose stated purpose was to regulate the industry, establishing minimum commissions, uniform fees, and to provide a listing service for sellers. In reality, the VREB's intent was to crowd out the hordes of low-level speculators cutting into their profits. One unfortunate result of the government's lax regulatory approach was that, despite the CPR and VIC's virtual duopoly, the real estate market threatened to descend into a free-for-all, with hungry brokers from all over the country fighting for a bigger slice of the pie. Establishing minimum fees, reasoned members (including Walter Gravely, Henry Ceperly, and F.C. Innes), would stop smaller firms from undercutting them. A listing service would give them some measure of control over the flow of information. To keep out smaller businesses, the VREB made their membership prohibitively expensive. Members also had to be elected by a four-fifths majority, with a ceiling of only fifty members total.

The board lasted just four months.

Throughout that time, divisions arose over membership fees and commission splits. Members were found to be engaged in unethical buying and selling practices. One member in particular — D.F.

Douglas — was expelled from the organization for a secret speculation arrangement with a client.

In the meantime, Oppenheimer's influence continued to grow; in 1888, he became the president of the Vancouver Board of Trade. In 1889, he officially opened Stanley Park. As evidence of his social standing, he was one of the very few Jewish-Canadians admitted to membership at the whites-only Terminal City Club, and by 1891, two years after *The World*'s list was published, his personal assets had grown by more than a million dollars. Throughout the late 1880s and early 1890s — in his dual role as the city's chief magistrate and its largest property owner — he had been working furiously to promote VIC land east of District Lot 541 (which the CPR had set as Vancouver's new downtown core), and in so doing, had handed out a series of sweetheart deals to wealthy associates. Sugar Magnate B.T. Rogers was given a piece of donated land to build a refinery, as well as tax breaks, water exemptions, and a taxpayer-funded railway between the refinery and downtown.

A number of civic improvement projects followed, including sewers, water lines, and even electric streetlights (among the first in North America). But, as Oppenheimer and the real estate elite well knew, the most important venture would be the construction of a streetcar line. Like the road and highway systems that would later follow, the electric streetcar was capable of increasing property values like few other amenities could, immediately opening up vast tracts of uninhabited forest, so they could be subdivided and transformed into the suburbs of tomorrow.

And for those who had invested heavily in land, it was important that these suburbs sprung up on property they owned.

Mayor David Oppenheimer, circa 1891. Image courtesy of CVA.

In 1889, The Vancouver Electric Light and Rail Company was founded (counting among its directors Oppenheimer, J.W. Horne, Charles D. Rand, Jonathan Miller, CPR Superintendent Harry Abbott, and George and Hugh Keefer), and, unsurprisingly, won the bid to both light the city with electricity, and construct a thirteen-mile rail line. To entice the company toward their land holdings, the CPR granted it a series of subdivided lots in District Lot 526 (which they would soon christen "Fairview," and which also happened to be beside lots owned in part by VIC shareholder Israel Wood Powell). The CPR's grant to the VIC is indicative of the changing relationship between the railroad and the other faction of real estate oligarchs coming to dominate Vancouver's civic affairs. In fact, by the early 1890s, Oppenheimer and his associates — mostly hailing from the East End rather than the CPR-dominated West End — had begun to stand up to the railroad they had previously courted. They fought for safety crossings at railway lines. They challenged the CPR in court over right-of-ways on the waterfront. They increased property taxes. They even funded a competitor, granting a three hundred thousand dollar bonus to the CPR's main rival, the Northern Pacific Railway. This change in attitude was more than the railway was expecting, leading a frustrated Harry Abbott to remind aldermen in a meeting that Vancouver owed its property values "almost entirely [...] to the existence of the CPR."

Illustrative of this divide was the debate over the location of a new post office. By 1888, mail was being delivered to the offices of Ross and Ceperly (continuing Ross' tradition of being associated with the postal service), and when the city began looking for a more permanent location, the clash pitted Vancouver's two biggest landowners against one another. During a boisterous public meeting in March of 1890, representatives of the CPR and the VIC squared off, with the railroad arguing in favour of the downtown core, and the improvement company demanding that it be placed in their territory on Hastings Street. Property mogul Charles D. Rand was "loudly called for," reported the *Province*, and, in a surprise turn, took the floor in support of the Granville Street location. He claimed that "American towns are calling away our carpenters and other tradesmen," noting that Port Angeles, Tacoma, Seattle, Anacortes, and Cedro were booming while Vancouverites were "all divided against themselves: the east against the west." In the end, Rand urged the VIC (of which he was a shareholder) to "take what they could get ... it was the duty of every man to pull for this grand project."

In relatively short order, these petty squabbles wouldn't matter. Because, in 1893, Vancouver's housing market fell apart.

An economic depression had spread across much of the US and Canada in the mid-1890s, but in new, less resilient cities like Vancouver, its effects were even more pronounced. Suddenly, the speculators that the mayor and the VIC had so delicately cultivated packed up and fled with their money. A wave of bankruptcies followed, pushing local soup kitchens to capacity, and leading nearly four hundred people to seek refuge in squatter's shacks along the False Creek waterfront. Even the once-mighty CPR shuttered its land office. Luckily, thanks in part to measures adopted by the railway, the collapse wasn't as severe as in Winnipeg during the bust, but nonetheless, property values dropped significantly. During this period, Oppenheimer too saw his influence diminish. By 1891, his health was failing. His hand-picked successor, Fred Cope (Head of the Vancouver Builder's Association), won the mayoral election of 1892 by only eleven votes, and many aldermen were replaced by people less sympathetic to the interests of wealthy elites. During the bust of 1893, Oppenheimer Brothers had collapsed, and two years later, the Vancouver Electric Railway Company was sold to a firm based in London. At least one of his allies, J.W. Horne, had left council to become a provincial MLA. Like Oppenheimer, Vancouverites struggled through much of the mid-1890s, with the brunt of the depression borne by the working class. According to a particularly dire report given to the Vancouver Trades and Labour Council, the city's tradespeople — particularly those in the construction sector — were woefully underemployed. They also received little sympathy from those in power; in 1891, the Vancouver Board of Trade and the CPR called for the removal of the squatter's shacks along False Creek — a decision the Supreme Court delayed until the fall of 1893, and which Francis Carter-Cotton, formerly a journalist with the *News-Advertiser* and now an MLA, managed to further delay, bringing a petition before the legislature that contained over six hundred names. By 1896, half of the city's carpenters weren't working at all, while many others were forced to labour for substandard wages.

Vancouver's first property boom was over.

The city would ultimately recover, but not in Oppenheimer's lifetime; Vancouver's largest private landowner died on New Year's Eve, 1897, amongst the ruins of the housing market he had helped create, a day before he was due to turn sixty-six.

"In the passing away of David Oppenheimer," noted the *Vancouver Daily World*, "Vancouver loses ones of her staunchest friends, and one who has done more to advance her prosperity than any other individual [...] Few men have lived a busier or more useful life, and in years to come he will be remembered as one of the 'Fathers of Vancouver.'"

But even after Oppenheimer's passing, a new generation of developers and speculators were set to make the boom — and crash of the 1890s — seem tame by comparison. The twentieth century was just around the corner, and "Those Who Own the Earth" were about to make Vancouver's property market explode like never before.

6.

HERE COMES THE BOOM

*"There was a speculative movement in land
rising to a climax in Vancouver, something that
was to assume gigantic proportions in the
following 18 months. Already shoe clerks were
beginning to go without lunch to make
payments on plots of land in distant suburbs,
and to go about their duties dreaming of the
quick turnover and the long profit."*

— Bertrand Sinclair, *The Inverted Pyramid*, 1924

IN THE WAKE of the market collapse, Vancouver's political climate grew increasingly volatile.

While the economic divide between classes was much less pronounced than in other Canadian cities, the depression of the 1890s still served to exacerbate the tension between haves and have-nots, and the ensuing years saw an increased demand for working-class voices at City Hall. This was part of a broader trend toward econ-

omic reform that was sweeping across North American and Europe
— inspired in large part by influential economist Henry George — a
rejection of the rentier capitalism (a term describing profit made
through controlling access to property) epitomized by men like
Oppenheimer and the business elite. Land, George argued, not
labour, should be the primary source of government revenue, in the
form of a Single Land Tax on landowners.

"The tax upon land values is, therefore, the most just and equal of
all taxes," George had written, in his 1879 book *Progress and Poverty*.
"It falls only upon those who receive from society a peculiar and valuable benefit, and upon them in proportion to the benefit they receive.
It is the taking by the community, for the use of the community, of
that value which is the creation of the community. It is the application of the common property to common uses. When all rent is taken
by taxation for the needs of the community, then will the equality
ordained by Nature be attained. No citizen will have an advantage
over any other citizen save as is given by his industry, skill, and intelligence; and each will obtain what he fairly earns. Then, but not till
then, will labor get its full reward, and capital its natural return."

The single land tax was a concept which already enjoyed widespread support amongst economists (including Adam Smith and
Milton Friedman), and even such notables as Benjamin Franklin. In
particular, George argued, the tax would discourage speculation —
something he saw as contrary to the public good.

"Everybody works but the vacant lot," George once wrote. "I paid
$3600 for this lot and will hold 'till I get $6000. The profit is
unearned increment made possible by the presence of this community and enterprise of its people. I take the profit without earning it."

However, given that land was often in the possession of the
wealthy, themselves tied in with government, George's ideas found
few proponents at the policy level. During this period, Vancouver's
real estate industry had slowed to a virtual crawl; in 1897, the city's

Land Registry Office recorded only $5,500 in revenue. Few — if any — new faces appeared in real estate, and many prominent industry professionals, like Robert G. Tatlow and F.C. Innes, moved into other speculative ventures, like mining or timber. Charles D. Rand left the city altogether. While Fred Cope (Oppenheimer's successor) managed to hang on for a second term as mayor, before being replaced by real estate agent Robert Anderson, the industry's influence on council began to wane. As the 1890s marched on, the city's annual elections continued to be hostly contested, with an increasing divide between the desires of the wealthy, and the desires of the working class. A movement of reformers, led by Francis Carter-Cotton, organized to push the interests of merchants and small-business owners.

It got ugly.

When grocery merchant William Templeton ran for the mayoralty in 1897, he tried desperately to portray himself as a friend of the working man. In reality, Templeton was a CPR insider who had personally benefited from the original land grant, and his opponents were quick to paint him as an out-of-touch member of the business elite. While he managed to win the 1897 election, the harassment he subsequently suffered in the press (and in particular *The World*) was so extreme that after he lost his bid for reelection in 1898, he committed suicide.

Owing to global economic growth, and the stimulus provided by the Klondike Gold Rush, Vancouver's financial woes began to ease in the early part of the twentieth century. By 1901, the city's Land Registry Office reported revenues of almost $10,000 — nearly double what they had been four years earlier — and Vancouver, then a town of 26,000, boasted forty-six real estate firms. Growth remained slow, but reasonable through the early 1900s, and many of the city's mayors were merchants or other non-real-estate professionals. Speculation had even become something of a dirty word in the press.

"WE WANT HOMEBUILDERS," declared an ad in *The Vancouver*

Daily Province in June of 1906. "Not Speculators, as only about thirty lots are in this division, so come early and secure yours and give your youngsters the chance to have their cheeks browned by the Southern airs blowing over the rippling waters of the Gulf and the Pacific Ocean, their lungs strengthened, and their eyes brightened."

Although real estate's power in the city was diminished, it was by no means defeated. As Vancouver expanded, landowners continued to open up new areas for development, including the nearby municipality of Point Grey, and much of that property was quickly snapped up by wealthy industry insiders. In the autumn of 1906, some $86,650 worth of Point Grey property was purchased at auction in a single afternoon, by realtors who handily outbid individual buyers (property speculator C.T. Dunbar, wrote *The Daily Province*, "caused cold chills to run up and down the spinal column of would-be acreage buyers" when he opened the bidding on two three-acre lots at a whopping $5000).

And then, in 1909, the measured growth which had characterized the decade thus far vanished, and the city — indeed, the entire province — descended into speculative insanity. The market explosion that followed was the result of several intersecting factors — chief among those, the crushing victory of Richard McBride's Conservative government in the provincial legislature. The party had been in power since 1903, and had spent years using free-market rhetoric to disguise their true intentions: advancing the interests of the financial elite. Chief among their allies were the wealthy speculators and rentier capitalists descending on the provincial housing market — most of them from Europe and the United States. Even before 1909, the Conservatives had redrafted the provincial Land Act, allowing real estate professionals to get around government preemption limits by collecting land on behalf of others, and then reselling it (this required nothing more than a signature, and stories abounded of speculators buying beer for anyone who would sign a power of attorney form). The province, Attorney General William Bowser argued, would vehemently defend the "freedom of the speculator," encouraging them to buy, sell, and hyper-inflate the value of land in an environment virtually free of oversight.

"The Government cannot control the investments the people wish to make any more than it can undertake to regulate the food that they eat or the clothes they wear," Bowser claimed. "As matter of fact, these speculative waves come and go, and, especially on this coast, have succeeded each other many times [...] When Governments dictate to the people what they shall buy and sell and how and at what prices, they will be about as successful as our ministerial friends in making everybody good according to their standard of goodness."

And investors responded.

Between 1908 and 1913, the rate at which overseas capital flowed into BC real estate increased by a staggering 1,175 per cent — much of that focused around or within Vancouver. During this period, real-estate interests also managed to wrest back control of city council; between 1904 and 1915, they accounted for anywhere between thirty to fifty per cent of its aldermen. In 1909, the same year as the Conservatives took much of the legislature, Vancouver elected realtor Charles Stanford Douglas as its mayor, a man who, according to *The World*, "had accumulated property by fair means." By 1910, the city was home to more than six hundred real estate agents. By 1912, there would be more than one thousand — one for every hundred citizens. Overseas money poured in, encouraged by the wealthy and their enablers in government, as well as a series of local lending institutions set up chiefly to finance land deals (virtually all of these, including Dominion Stock and Bond Corporation, and Vancouver, Savings, Loan, Trust, and Guarantee Co, were operated by McBride MLAS or real estate developers like Henry Ceperly). A series of notable public buildings also took shape, including the provincial courthouse (later the Vancouver Art Gallery), the Birks Building and the Vancouver

Block. During the 1909–1913 period, speculator influence was so great that it even influenced the naming of major streets; in 1909, in hopes of encouraging American investors to purchase land near Westminster Avenue and Ninth Street, the city renamed them Main Street and Broadway, respectively. In 1911, the CPR opened up Shaughnessy for development (but with specific covenants inserted to restrict ownership to solely the white and affluent). The first apartments began to appear in the West End, and prefab bungalows sprung up in Kitsilano. The city made thirteen million dollars in building permits during 1910 alone. By 1912, that number had grown to nineteen million. Naturally, land values had skyrocketed; a fifty-two-foot lot on Hastings, which sold for twenty-six thousand dollars in 1904, had jumped to ninety thousand dollars by 1908. By 1909, it was $175,000. In 1912, at a time when wages were roughly fifty cents an hour, a lot at the corner of Granville and Hastings sold for an incredible $725,000.

But, as was typical during the McBride years, these figures represented a gain for speculators, and a loss for locals. Theoretically, the government claimed, cheap land was available province-wide to anyone who wanted it, in the form of preemptions — of the sort that had allowed the Three Greenhorns to gain a foothold in the West End. But in reality, preemptor maps drawn up by the Department of Lands showed that the majority of that property had already been gobbled up by syndicates of investors from New York, Chicago, and London — syndicates in bed with the government, who had quietly bought the land at below-market rates. By this time, many members of McBride's government were also speculating themselves; Price Ellison, the aptly-named Finance Minister, was president of Dominion Stock and Bond, having worked a deal to buy land from the government at one dollar an acre, and sell it for almost forty dollars (using the profits to construct the Dominion Building — then the tallest building in the British Empire — which still stands today). A company run by Attorney General Bowser was up to its neck in land leases, and at one point, to keep up with payments, he introduced a bill in the legislature to artificially depress the value of his own property. By then, speculative mania had even descended down to the working class, and eager Vancouverites stretched themselves to the breaking point to cash in on the boom; according to a 1912 pamphlet entitled "The Crisis in B.C." during a single week in October, more than forty per cent of the land-purchase applications received were from working class people.

"Great is the confidence of the participants — and the entire community participates," wrote novelist Bertrand Sinclair, of the boom. "For the time being it is forgotten that whatever goes up must come down. It is a great game while it lasts. Better than draw poker. Better than playing the ponies. It is legitimate, respectable, as well as thrilling. It isn't gambling. It isn't even speculation. It is investment."

"We live in the land of destiny," beamed one R.J. McDougall, in a 1911 issue of *B.C. Magazine*. "In the land of wealth where, though gold is not idly picked off the rocks or from the pavements in the streets, it is just as surely gained from the platted acres and twenty-footers around us. One day an artisan may put the scanty savings of a lifetime into a tiny holding out among the evergreens, and on the morrow almost, he is building city blocks from the proceeds thereof."

For nearly four years, global capital flowed into the city, fuelling a cycle of rapid expansion, population growth, and a property market that had surged completely out of control. In 1912, at the height of the boom, McBride was elected for another term. But despite maintaining a cheery outlook in the press, there were many within the government who were beginning to worry about what might happen when the bubble burst.

"It was all a glorious daydream," McBride's personal secretary R.E. Gosnell later wrote, "from which I felt, sooner or later, we must awake to sterner realities."

And awake they did.

"Warnings that the McBride empire rested on a base of loose sand, that real development was confused with speculative dreaming, that freedom had been established only for the speculator, that the fruits of the toil of workers were consumed by greedy buccaneers, were dismissed as the sour complaints of gloomy political pedlars," historian Martin Robin later wrote. "Bowser, who cared little about the rule of law or the concept of justice, spoke for the speculator, the prevailing culture hero who pursued profit by utterly disregarding accepted rules, just as McBride was worshipped by the myriad of dreamers for his facile optimism, his capacity for ignoring rights and looking the other way."

In 1913, a committee of British investors toured the western province, and they didn't like what they saw. Further jarred by the crash of the US stock market, they, and many other speculators began to pull up stakes, and the result was catastrophic. McBride's strategy, while giving the appearance of economic growth, had instead allowed speculative profits to replace actual labour and industry, and without those profits, both the economy and the housing market went into a tailspin. Building permits, which had topped nineteen million dollars in 1912, plummeted to less than one million dollars by 1915. Government revenues fell by half. Commercial rents declined by fifty per cent, and the working-class investors who had tried to claw their way into the market were forced into bankruptcy. In 1914, Dominion Trust collapsed, leaving its more than five thousand creditors with nothing. The City of South Vancouver went into receivership. By the winter of 1913, the city had spent $150,000 on unemployment relief, and construction had slowed to a virtual standstill. And in the wake of it, property values fell substantially; a corner lot on Cambie and Broadway, listed for ninety thousand dollars, eventually sold for less than eight thousand dollars.

People were "perceptibly poorer in pocket and prosperity and speculation got a terrible jar." wrote R.E. Gosnell. "There was everything to sell and nothing to buy."

The crash destroyed the Conservative government. In the aftermath, it was discovered that Attorney General Bowser, unable to meet his mortgage obligations, had introduced a bill which allowed his company to postpone their payments indefinitely. He had also helped Dominion Trust (run by Finance Minister Price Ellison) circumvent government banking regulations. Both Bowser and McBride had appointed siblings to lucrative government posts. In 1915, Ellison, Provincial Secretary H.E. Young, and Premier McBride himself all resigned in scandal.

The bubble had burst in a catastrophic way. The "Land of Destiny" had gone to ruin, the "scanty savings" of artisans long vanished, and for the moment, Vancouverites found themselves more firmly in the world of Henry George than R.J. MacDougall.

After five years of spectacular returns, the vacant lot wasn't working. And the next few decades wouldn't be easy.

INTERLUDE:
Real Estate And Race (Part I)

Chang Toy had taken a gamble.

It was a speculative investment in the future — specifically, his own. The year was 1912, and in the four decades since first arriving in BC, the merchant prince of Chinatown had done well for himself; landing in New Westminster as a humble labourer, he had worked his way up to being one of Vancouver's most successful businessmen. By the early part of the twentieth century, he had amassed a considerable fortune, and — as was customary for wealthy men back in China — taken five wives. His business reach extended into all aspects of the Chinese and European communities, including fish-packing plants, money lending, import/export contracts, and of course, real estate.

And by 1912, one particular piece of real estate was giving him trouble — or more precisely, what was left of one.

Less than a year earlier, the City of Vancouver had voted to widen Pender Street, a process that required the expropriation of several Chinatown properties, including Chang's grocery warehouse at the corner of Pender and Carrall Streets. The warehouse, built on a standard-sized lot, had been purchased in 1903, and in the ensuing years, had served as an unofficial gathering place for new Chinese arrivals in Vancouver — particularly those from the Poon Yue region of Guangdong province, where Chang had spent his childhood. Exercising imminent domain, the city had paid Chang sixty-two thousand dollars for the property, and in return, left him with a virtually useless six-foot-wide strip of land next to the sidewalk. For many business owners, this would have been the end of the story; the two most obvious answers were to leave the lot vacant, or sell it to the owner next door, to allow them to expand their business.

But Chang had other plans.

He had recently found himself in a disagreement with a wealthy business associate (one whose name hasn't been recorded). This associate insisted the land was useless. Chang disagreed. So, the pair had made a wager to the tune of ten thousand dollars (about a quarter of a million dollars today). And then Chang got to work. He was no stranger to property development; one of the first Chinese-Canadians to buy land in Chinatown, he owned ten properties in the neighbourhood, and at least five more elsewhere in the city. And at Chang's level, real estate appears to have been colour-blind; his non-Chinatown businesses were hotels or rooming houses, all of which served a predominantly white clientele. This was an exceedingly rare achievement for a Chinese-Canadian. Historically, Chinese-Canadians found themselves subject to all manner of racism and discrimination at the hands of white society and countless times over the past 130 years, real estate was employed as a tool to advance a racist agenda.

Even before the completion of the CPR — an operation which brought some seventeen thousand Chinese workers to Canada (hired because they could be paid much less, and used for much more dangerous work than their white counterparts) — the provincial government had passed legislation banning anyone of Chinese descent from purchasing Crown land. Technically, Chinese-Canadians could still buy from private landowners, but before 1900, virtually all the land in Chinatown was owned by white speculators, and either rented or leased by Chinese-Canadians. Chinatowns themselves sprung up anywhere that new Chinese-Canadian settlers landed — with the largest in Victoria and Vancouver — in part out of a desire to keep themselves separate from a European culture that was hostile to their presence, and in part because their characteristically low wages only allowed them to settle in areas considered too downmarket for white immigrants. However, as an extra guarantee against the small, but wealthy, Chinese merchant class, Europeans in upscale neighbourhoods like Shaughnessy would specifically insert covenants into their land title documents, barring private sale to members of other ethnic groups.

At the time of incorporation, Vancouver's Chinatown was home to ninety permanent residents, virtually all of them former CPR labourers who found themselves in the Terminal City with no work and few economic prospects. Through the late nineteenth and early twentieth century, Vancouver absorbed eighty-six per cent of Canada's new Asian arrivals; and although the actual increase in the Chinese-Canadian population was relatively small (they made up only seven per cent of BC's population before 1911), fears of a Chinese takeover spread quickly through the white community.

And it just as quickly led to violence.

The city's first race riot, in January of 1887, was the result of tensions over both race and real estate; after the CPR hired a crew of Chinese-Canadian workers to clear company land in the West

End, paying them roughly half the wage offered to Europeans, a group of white labourers chased the clearing crew out of town with torches while singing "John Brown's Body," a song which, strangely, is a blistering rebuke of racism. Later in the same year, Mayor Malcolm McLean won a second term by capitalizing on this growing anger, making a campaign promise to further restrict the property rights of Chinese Canadians. By 1907, white Vancouverites had formed the Asiatic Exclusion League (a branch of a similar organization formed in the US), and papers such as the *Sun*, *Daily Province*, and *Saturday Sunset* regularly featured racist cartoons and editorials discussing the "Chinese Problem" Provincially, the cause had found a champion in Premier Richard McBride, who told the legislature in 1919 that he was committed to "a white British Columbia, a white land, and a white Empire."

"We do not mean to be offensive to our Asian neighbours," he continued. "It is not a question of race against race. But because of economic and social conditions, we the white people of this country insist on our right to say we will conserve this country for our own race."

Into the mid-twentieth century, Chinatown remained a world separate from white Vancouver. Indeed, most European Canadians stayed out of the area altogether, except to take advantage of Chinese merchants, many of whom gave out gifts during the annual Chinese New Year celebrations. Among the many complaints of European settlers were the overcrowded and unsanitary conditions that prevailed throughout much of the neighbourhood; beginning in the early 1900s, the city health inspector began sending regular delegations through Chinatown, and the Provincial Board of Health unsuccessfully attempted to institute annual inspections of all Chinese-occupied dwellings.

And on those two points, they were right: Chinatown was

class), Vancouver was also home to one more distinct ethnic enclave: Japantown.

While Japanese immigrants had been arriving in BC since the late 1870s, it was in much smaller numbers than their Chinese-Canadian counterparts, and they experienced very different forms of discrimination. Where Chinese-Canadians were forced to pay a "head tax" upon entry into Canada, Japan was bound by a 1907 "Gentleman's Agreement," which limited immigration by diplomatic means. Where the head tax effectively restricted a woman's ability to immigrate from China, and thus start families, no such limitations were placed on the movement of Japanese women. But after the 1923 passage of the Chinese Exclusion Act, BC's Chinese-Canadian population dropped off sharply, and following the outbreak of World War II, Vancouver's white racists turned their attention toward the residents of Japantown — by then a thriving community of some ten thousand people, settled near Powell, Main, Cordova, and Alexander streets. The push for Japanese Internment — in camps strewn throughout the BC interior — was largely spearheaded by Vancouver-area politicians, including Ian Mackenzie, federal MP for Vancouver Centre.

"It is the government's plan to get these people out of BC as fast as possible," Mackenzie later explained. "It is my personal intention, as long as I remain in public life, to see they never come back here. Let our slogan be for British Columbia: 'No Japs from the Rockies to the seas.'"

At Mackenzie's urging, and despite a total lack of credible intell' gence, Ottawa convened the Standing Committee on Orientals British Columbia, a group composed mostly of white racists, in ing New Westminster Mayor Fred Hume. Hume was partir vociferous in his condemnation of Japanese-Canadians, mending their immediate deportation and imprisonmer crowded. And it was filthy. No accurate count was kept of the Asian population in early city directories (any address with Chinese-Canadian residents simply read "Oriental"), but surveys by the city health department found that the vast majority of rooming houses in Chinatown were packed well above capacity. Some — including Chang Toy's "Oriental Hotel" — were even demolished for repeated health code violations. In 1902, Health Inspector Robert Marrion discovered that every one of the Armstrong Lodging House's twenty-seven rooms was occupied by more than six people.

"The places where Chinese people lived were small and over-crowded," noted a 1908 city report. "They'd cram 4 bunkbeds into a small room. All the cooking was done on a wood-burner and there were never enough pots and pans."

But while overcrowding was the result of Chinese labourers' desire to send home as much of their meagre wages as possible, the neighbourhood's unsanitary nature had much more to do with its white landowners than its Chinese-Canadian residents. Up to that point, the city hadn't bothered to install plumbing in China-town, and by the summer of 1903, conditions had become so dire that Chinese-Canadian property owners on Dupont Street offered to fund their construction through increased property taxes. The tax increase was loudly rejected by white landowners, and con-struction languished for a further two years, until Health Inspector Underhill personally petitioned the city works department.

Despite this blatant racism, BC was a reasonably cosmopolitan place during the first part of the twentieth century, with more than half of its pre-World War II population born outside the province. And although rich neighbourhoods like Shaughnessy and the Brit-ish Properties had managed to legally turn themselves into whites-only communities (property title documents also forbade the construction of apartments, to keep out the poor and middle-one contemporary observer to note that the committee "spoke of the Japanese-Canadians in the way that the Nazis would have spoken about Jewish-Germans."

The Internment argument was espoused by only a select few during the early 1940s, including Vancouver Alderman Halford Wilson, whom Ottawa's wartime censorship board deemed so extreme, that they regularly removed his comments from local newspapers.

"[C]ompetent authorities are satisfied [that the] security situation is well in hand and are confident of the correct and loyal behaviour of Canadian residents of Japanese origin," Prime Minister Mackenzie King told BC, during a December 1941 radio address.

"[A] good deal of the agitation for the removal of the Japanese had nothing whatever to do with the war or the necessities of defence," added *The Daily Province*, in February of 1942, "but was promoted by agencies that had political axes to grind or selfish interests to serve."

However, after the bombing of Pearl Harbour, fears of a Japanese invasion spread through BC's white community, and suddenly, Ottawa found itself deluged with letters and petitions from private citizens, and civic organizations.

"The presence of thousands of Japanese on the Pacific coast adds enormously to the dangers of hostile attacks which may be made very soon," wrote the Vancouver Real Estate Exchange. "It is generally recognized that it is the intention of many of the Japanese to support their countrymen in the event of an invasion."

Eventually, Mackenzie King conceded, and the standing committee got its wish; in February of 1942, more than twenty thousand Japanese Canadians were removed to the Interior, and their property was confiscated by the Office of the Custodian of Enemy Property. While Ottawa initially agreed to hold on to possessions and real estate, aggressive lobbying on the part of BC politicians (including Vancouver alderman Halford Wilson) led them to change their minds. In a matter of months, the government began "liquidating" Japanese-Canadian assets, and selling them to white British Columbians at bargain prices. The city was overjoyed, noting, in multiple issues of the *Sun* and *Daily Province*, their plan to "reclaim" Japantown for "white habitation."

"Without fuss or friction, a change that may have a significant bearing on British Columbia's future is taking place in Vancouver," the *Sun* reported. "The Japanese are moving out, and Canadians are moving in. There are new faces behind the counters in establishments formerly operated by Nipponese, and it is expected their number will increase as the exodus from the coast gathers momentum."

Interned Japanese-Canadians were devastated. Close to one thousand letters were written and sent to Ottawa, all of them expressing shock and betrayal, citing charitable and community contributions, and begging for the right to retain their homes.

All of them were ignored.

"This property is our home," BC resident Toyo Takahashi wrote, in the spring of 1944, "a reward for long years of toil and anticipation, a source of recreation, a stake in the future [...] and an insurance for our later welfare. My husband is now too advanced in years to earn a livelihood, his health is beginning to fail, and is looking forward to retirement next year. After all our efforts in good citizenship we do not deserve to have our retirement jeopardized by the liquidation of our properties."

"Surely there must be a terrible mistake somewhere!" added Japanese-Canadian citizen Macer Okamoto. "I can't even imagine any possible reason for our property being confiscated. It would be different if my father happened to be a Japanese National (an enemy alien) but if you will take the trouble to look up the records, you will find that he is a naturalized Canadian citizen [...] Doesn't his naturalization papers mean anything?"

In 1986, a Price Waterhouse audit concluded that the losses to Japanese Canadians exceeded four hundred million dollars.

Exterior of the Sam Kee Building, 1936
(CVA AM54-S4-: Bu P255.7)

Unlike many others, Chang Toy's wealth and status seem to have allowed him to escape some of the institutional racism that pervaded BC society during his career. During the 1907 race riot, he had been well-connected enough that he managed to send his sons to stay with a pair of white business associates. In that same year, his company was one of just four Chinatown businesses clearing more than $150,000 in annual profit (a figure six times greater than most of his contemporaries). Even the expropriation of his warehouse doesn't seem to have been motivated by any discernible racism (plenty of buildings owned by white Vancouverites had to be purchased and demolished for the same project), and during the purchase process, Chang's shrewd negotiation skills allowed him to sell the property at market rate (he advised his attorneys to start at seventy thousand dollars, before settling for the sixty-two thousand he knew the lot was worth).

And then, in 1913, he scored another win.

Contacting the architecture firm of Bryan and Gillam, Chang had commissioned a building for what remained of his Pender Street lot. Measuring just six feet in depth, it included a double-sized basement, and bay windows on the second floor, effectively doubling his square footage. And because the architects themselves carried out the work, construction was completed for approximately eight thousand dollars — meaning Chang actually made money on the initial wager. When the work was done, he named it after the pseudonymous head of his business empire: the Sam Kee Building. Today, it still stands on the corner of Pender and Carrall Streets, and holds the Guinness World Record for the narrowest commercial building in the world (this honour would likely have horrified the Guinness family of the day; their British Properties development in North Vancouver was among the region's most high-profile whites-only neighbourhoods).

In 1978, the BC government amended the Land Title Act to prohibit the enforcement of race-based covenants, however, thousands of them still remain on the books today.

TERMINAL CITY
(1914 – 1946)

"Why should a piece of empty real estate be sacrosanct? Is the owner's right to keep it vacant superior to the right of local families to have a roof over their heads? Any public representative who answers 'yes' to that question is not only out of sympathy with humanity but out of step with social progress."

— ***The Vancouver Sun***, December 27, 1944

7.

THE OCCUPATION

"Vancouver is facing a housing crisis. Real Estate agents have difficulty in finding apartments and houses to accommodate hundreds of people seeking quarters every day — soldiers' families, war workers, and people who are swelling the city's population."

— *Vancouver News-Herald*, 1941

IT WAS A COLD, snowy Saturday in January of 1946, and Bob McEwan decided he'd had enough.

Along with thirty-five other members of New Veterans Branch 163, he had spent the afternoon at the Legion Hall on Seymour Street, discussing the city's housing shortage — one which had been steadily building over the past twenty-five years, and had, following the return of soldiers after World War II, assumed crisis proportions. It was 2:30 in the afternoon by the time McEwan and his compatriots crossed Georgia Street in the direction of the Hotel Vancouver. For nearly eight years it had stood vacant, its furniture and bedding cleared out in advance of a date with the wrecker's ball. In the face of the housing shortage, it had been suggested as a temporary hostel by several civic and charity groups, but thus far, arguments over funding and jurisdiction had produced no meaningful action.

McEwan was about to change that.

Having returned from the front in late 1945, he, like many veterans, had been unable to find accommodation, and was instead forced to move back in with his parents. Unfortunately, his father's two-room apartment was less than luxurious, forcing him onto a couch in the kitchen (it was such a tight squeeze that he had to sleep with his head in the gas oven). He had already attended numerous meetings about the city's housing shortage, and, alongside several other veterans, had been involved in a public protest on the lawn of the city courthouse — one stifled by police before it could garner much attention. But in the several weeks since, McEwan and the others had devised a plan that would make them impossible to ignore. Approaching the front gate, McEwan strolled calmly up to the single army guard posted outside and said: "We're taking over the Hotel Vancouver, so sit tight." Standing over six feet tall, and weighing 220 pounds, McEwan wasn't the sort of man to be argued with. Back in 1940, he had enlisted in the army at sixteen, after lying about his age, and spent four years fighting in the European theatre alongside the Seaforth Highlanders. Wounded in 1944, he nonetheless returned to the front as part of a mortar platoon, making his way through Italy, France, Belgium, Holland, and Germany.

The guard didn't put up a fight, and within three hours, the building had taken on the air of a military operation; veterans brought in bed frames, mattresses, and blankets borrowed from division headquarters. A female officer took on the role of room clerk, providing new arrivals with a room assignment, and a square of cardboard on which to write their name. A food committee prepared sandwiches for lunch. McEwan and a small committee drew up a code of conduct, urging occupants: "It is vital to the success of this emergency act and to the good name of the Legion that the administration and conduct of the hotel be above reproach...Any irrational conduct on your part will lose us the goodwill of the general public."

After years of neglect, the building itself was in appalling condition, with missing light fixtures, doors torn from hinges, and broken plumbing. Nonetheless, as the day went on, the initial group of thirty-five had swelled to more than one hundred, and by nightfall, the hotel's Spanish Ballroom was the site of a boisterous party. A banner hung across the front entrance reading: "Action at Last Veterans! Rooms For You. Come and Get Them."

Despite a police presence at the scene, no attempt was made to remove the protestors (known in the pages of the *Daily Province* as the "Army of Occupation"). In fact, the action was immediately met with support by locals, the press, the Vancouver Trades and Labour Council, and even the government.

"You did right," said North Vancouver MP James Sinclair, in the pages of the *Sun*. "You waited until all negotiations had failed, then you took the bull by the horns and moved in."

Over the course of the next day, more than seven hundred veterans and their spouses streamed in to register for rooms. Local merchants donated leftover food, meals, and coffee. Officials including Mayor James Cornett, and federal Veterans Affairs Minister Ian Mackenzie stopped by to investigate. Within three days, Mackenzie had agreed to provide seventy thousand dollars to operate the building as a veteran's hostel. The city provided twenty-five thousand dollars.

Ultimately, the Army of Occupation remained in the building for more than a year. Thanks to the direct action of McEwan and his fellow veterans, city council and the federal Department of Reconstruction and Supply (established for returning servicemen) agreed to provide permanent rental housing in a six hundred-unit subdivision known as Renfrew Heights. Together, they had challenged all three levels of government, carved out a place for themselves and their families, and found a solution to a housing shortage that had been plaguing the city for decades.

The reprieve would prove to be temporary.

8.

BETTER

"*Vancouver has more families than there is living space for. Many of these groups are jammed in with friends or relatives and all at the mercy of the landlords [...] Every apartment house is filled and many have long lists. Medium sized, and priced, houses are greatly in demand.*"

— *Vancouver Sun*, October 26, 1919

THE HOUSING CRISIS that prompted Bob McEwan and the New Veterans to occupy the Hotel Vancouver had its roots in the immediate aftermath of the 1913 market crash. In the years that followed, the city went through two small booms and one long bust, but even before that, citizens were already feeling the squeeze of an acute rental housing shortage. As of 1911, the city was home to 100,000 people, and during those years, between one-quarter and one-third of the working population rented — and of that, close to fifteen per cent were living in crowded or substandard housing. Many of these buildings were in the West End; by 1911, as the CPR opened Shaughnessy up to development, many of the neighbourhood's well-to-do residents migrated to Vancouver's posh new district, and in the aftermath of their departure, their homes were converted — after being sold, or by their original owners — into multi-family rooming houses for the working class. In Mount Pleasant, Fairview, and other East End districts, new immigrants — many of them Italian-Canadian — found themselves in similar circumstances, packed into converted homes originally intended for much smaller families. Since his appointment in 1904, Dr. Frederick Underhill, the city health inspector, had been appalled by the substandard conditions foisted upon lower-income Vancouverites, and in 1911, he appointed a lodging house and restaurant inspector in hopes of getting a handle on the situation.

He didn't like what he saw.

In 1911, the city had issued 480 licenses for lodging houses. Many of these were run by female landladies, often on behalf of property owners who cared very little for the upkeep of their buildings. The inspector's report detailed multiple unsanitary dwellings — many without adequate light or ventilation. Stoves in a number of houses were dangerously leaky, to the point where gas poisoning was common. And as the housing boom continued, conditions only got worse. Between 1905 and 1915, rents in Vancouver rose by more than forty per cent, quickly surpassing those in Toronto or Montreal. By 1912, as the bubble burst, and people lost their homes, the health department discovered sixty-two shacks had been built on land near City Hall. These shacks housed an astonishing fifteen hundred people — more than one hundred of them children — and of those dwellings, Underhilll concluded, three-quarters were grotesquely substandard. By 1913, the number of lodging house licenses had jumped from 480 to more than twenty-five hundred, and things had grown so dire that the Vancouver Council of Women drafted a letter to the city, begging them to solve the housing crisis before it got any worse. They were soon joined by a number of other organizations, including the Communist Party of Canada, the Family Welfare Bureau of Greater Vancouver, the University Women's League, and even the Vancouver Trades and Labour Council. Desperate, Dr. Underhill tried to introduce a universal safety and sanitation bylaw that would apply to all rental housing, but his efforts were halted by the outbreak of World War I.

Even after the war, real estate remained in a slump.

Construction slowed to a crawl during the war years, with an average of only one million dollars in building permits issued annually (compared with nineteen million at the peak of the boom). The crunch grew more acute after 1918, thanks to a hike in interest rates, a materials shortage, and the influx of returning soldiers. During the 1920s, the city's health department commissioned three different studies on overcrowding in Vancouver's lodging houses, and in 1919, a report of the Royal Commission of Industrial Relations stated that, more than virtually anything else, the labour unrest that was then sweeping BC was being exacerbated by a lack of sufficient housing. At roughly the same time, Vancouver's well-to-do were financing some of the city's most opulent structures, including the second Hotel Vancouver, The Ritz, and the Hotel Georgia, and in their attempts to reinvigorate the market, leading industry voices began to sound increasingly tone-deaf. By the time of the 1921 census, a whopping sixty-five per cent of Vancouver's population was renting (compared to fifty-three per cent in Toronto), virtually all of them in single-family homes. At the same time, those same detached homes made up eighty-eight per cent of the city's housing stock, indicating a growing divide between the working class and the wealthier absentee owners from whom they rented. Nonetheless, at a time when unemployment was above twenty per cent, and building costs had risen by more than fifty per cent, the real estate industry took to the pages of local papers and national journals, pushing home ownership as the only solution to the postwar depression.

"[It] teaches thrift and sobriety," read an industry-sponsored article in the *BC Record,* "it makes better and more contented citizens and eliminates that prey of unrest and radicalism — discontented rent-payers."

The industry did everything they could to push home ownership as a priority; the Western Retail and Lumberman's Association produced glossy catalogues like *Better Buildings*, which posited that: "The individual's standing in the community is influenced by the exterior appearance and surroundings of his home. The first impression received is usually a lasting one. One is labelled as having good taste or bad; as being progressive or indifferent; as being worthwhile or the reverse; through the appearance of his home."

"Better Buildings," the catalogue stated, were "'Better' in exterior appearance, in construction, in interior arrangement, and 'better' in the little things that make for comfort, convenience and economy of labour around the house. 'Better Buildings' need not necessarily mean more expensive buildings."

They even tried framing it as a patriotic duty.

"'Build a Home First,'" urged the June 1919 issue of *Western Lumberman.* "That's what the Government wants you to do because a revival of building activity will help the nation back to a peace basis quicker than any other thing. You did your part to help to win the war — now do all you can to help us get back to a peace basis."

And of course, there were the familiar supply-side arguments that would characterize the industry's position for decades.

"[W]on't the law of supply and demand solve the housing situation?" asked a 'reporter' in an advertorial in an October issue of the *Vancouver Sun.*

"That," replied his subject, "is the only way it will ever be solved."

In this case, it solved nothing.

In fact, the market proved so ill-equipped to provide homes for low-income earners, that in 1919, the federal government reluctantly implemented the Better Housing Scheme (BHS), in hopes of providing veterans with the assistance they so sorely needed. This decision, made by acting Prime Minister Thomas White, was motivated less by compassion for veterans than it was by the labour unrest simmering in most major Canadian cities, and the resulting rise in communist rhetoric. Given the urgency of the situation, the scheme was passed under the War Measures Act (meaning it required no parliamentary debate), and a committee was quickly formed, which included housing and labour activist Newton Rowell, town planner Thomas Adams, and early Vancouver speculator Gideon Robertson, who had since moved up to become Minister of Labour.

A building/real estate advertisement in an issue of
Western Lumberman, June 16, 1919.

Housing, noted the committee's 1919 report, "touches vitally the health, morals and general well-being of the entire community and its relation to the welfare of the returned soldiers and their families." The program would "promote the erection of dwelling houses of modern character to relieve congestion of population in cities and towns; to put within the reach of all working men, particularly returned soldiers, the opportunity of acquiring their own homes at actual cost of the building and land acquired at a fair value, thus eliminating the profits of the speculator; to contribute to the general health and wellbeing [sic] of the community by encouraging suitable town planning and housing schemes."

In concept, the program was surprisingly progressive; the government would make loans to each province, which the province would then extend to individual homebuyers. Interest was five per cent, repayable over a twenty-year period, and preference was given to ex-servicemen, or people of modest means (in this case, making a maximum of three thousand dollars per annum). It also imposed minimum standards for sanitation and space, and gave bonuses to families who stayed in their homes for more than ten years. Key in the development of the project was Canadian Town Planning Commission advisor Thomas Adams. Adams, a proponent of the "garden city" movement, with extensive planning experience in England, had already visited Vancouver back in 1909, declaring that it suffered from "haphazard growth and speculation in real estate," and urging city council to discard its geometric grid system of lots and single, detached homes in favour of larger properties and semi-detached houses (in this case, town houses or row houses, both of which were substantially cheaper).

"[I]t is recommended that, where possible, comparatively large sites should be acquired, by the method of expropriation, if necessary," the report continued, "so that those principles of town-planning may be applied which have received world-wide recognition as not only the most radical means of preventing slum development, but as the best and most economical means of providing working families with living conditions — gardens, open spaces, playgrounds for children and sun-lit rooms — such as have hitherto been usually the privilege of the rich."

City council wouldn't have it.

Though BC was the first province in Canada to utilize the

scheme, entrenched real estate interests at City Hall (Harry Gale, the mayor from 1918 to 1921, was a prominent real estate promoter) managed to redirect Ottawa's money to serve their own ends. At the urging of aldermen, the city rejected many of the report's recommendations, rejecting semi-detached housing in favour of craftsman-style bungalows on existing private, subdivided lots. This decision — alongside Ottawa's choice to set the annual salary ceiling at three thousand dollars per annum (the average working-class Vancouverite made twelve hundred to fifteen hundred dollars) automatically meant that many of the loans approved went to buyers who could afford a home without government help. Even worse, the homes built through the scheme mostly sold at market rates — well beyond the reach of the (in many cases unemployed) veterans for whom they had been intended. Some even sold for more; in 1919, a six-room bungalow in Mount Pleasant was listed in the pages of the *Sun* for $3,150. A BHS bungalow in the same neighbourhood cost $3,500. In 1920, following the resignation of one of its chief proponents, Newton Rowell, and the subsequent election of William Lyon Mackenzie King, the scheme was scaled back. In 1924, it was cancelled altogether, and despite its progressive intentions, it was derided as a failure. With the election of Mackenzie King, government intervention in the housing market ended in any meaningful form until the mid-1940s, with the prime minister pushing a market-oriented solution over "a general policy of socialism."

Ultimately, only 153 BHS homes were ever built in Vancouver.

The program — and its similarly reactive, ad hoc successors — failed those it endeavoured to help, and even many of its initial recipients; by 1938, with the Great Depression in full swing, half of all BHS homeowners had either defaulted, or were seriously delinquent in their payments, forcing the city to assume their loans, and making a subsequent generation of aldermen skittish about government intervention in low-cost housing. That said, it did, for the first time, bring together a series of progressive voices — both inside and outside of government — who would spend the decades ahead fighting for housing justice. This would include debates over sanitation and standard-of-living bylaws, comprehensive zoning, the establishment of city planning, a national housing registry, subsidized and social housing, and would ultimately culminate in the creation of the Canada Mortgage and Housing Corporation.

But for the people of Vancouver, things were going to get worse before they got any better.

9.

WELCOME TO THE JUNGLE

"Housing is becoming a social necessity of proportions which must be recognized as city-wide in their scope. When private enterprise cannot build homes at an economic rental, it then becomes the responsibility of the community to provide such shelter for the wage-earners in the lower income brackets."

— Alderman Helena Gutteridge, June 21, 1938

WHEN VANCOUVER ELECTED its first female alderman in March of 1937, the media treated it as little more than a curiosity.

"Although women have come to have a voice in the government of most of our cities, Vancouver people have hitherto refrained from entrusting them with such civic responsibilities," wrote the *Sun*. "Naturally, we cannot predict the course of Miss Gutteridge's civic career because we are unacquainted with her abilities and her tendencies. But in a general way we feel that the influence of a woman or women in the City Council is a wholesome one."

Sworn in wearing a navy blue dress, wire-rimmed glasses, and carrying a gift basket of snapdragons and tulips, the fifty-eight-year-old Helena Rose Gutteridge didn't look much like a radical. With close-cropped hair and a soft, British accent, she seemed more like a country schoolteacher than a civic politician — something the newspapers were quick to seize on; shortly before her swearing-in, a cartoon on the front page of the *Sun* (entitled "Good Grief! A Woman On City Council!") showed Gutteridge, looking demure and carrying a rolling pin, saying "Now, let's see — new curtains over there, flowers, ashtrays, and, er — language!"

Curtains were the least of Gutteridge's concerns.

For a start, she was a socialist — the third member of the far-left Cooperative Commonwealth Federation (CCF) elected to city council, handily defeating ex-alderman (and future nemesis) Henry L. Corey. She had also spent years as a labour activist, organizer, and suffragette, campaigning for better working hours and employee compensation in the garment trade. She had given impassioned speeches and hosted socialist radio shows. And for working Vancouverites, many of whom were crammed into increasingly substandard accommodation, she would soon become something of a champion.

She would also have her work cut out for her.

In the years following the collapse of the BHS, Vancouver's housing shortage had only gotten worse. Despite new innovations like the creation of a town planning council, and the commissioning of a citywide Master Plan, the ensuing mid-1920s building boom had been cut short by the Great Depression, and as the '30s dragged on, construction effectively came to a halt. In 1930, almost sixteen hundred building permits had been issued for new dwellings. By 1931, it was thirteen hundred. By 1934, it was only 190.

**Alderman Helena Gutteridge recites the oath of office,
March 30, 1937. Image courtesy of CVA.**

Adding to the crunch, only one element of the Vancouver Master
Plan, drafted by American engineering firm Harland Bartholomew
and Associates, had actually been adopted, and it only served to make
things worse: zoning. Vancouver was the first city in Canada to imple-
ment comprehensive zoning bylaws, based off of Bartholomew's vision
of a central commercial district surrounded by residential neighbourhoods. The idea, common in the emerging field of city planning, was to
protect outlying residential areas — and the single-family homes
therein — from inner-city urban blight and the encroachment of
slums, (common in many US and UK cities, and which comprised portions of Vancouver's Downtown East Side). Unfortunately, what the
bylaw did in practice was exacerbate the city's already severe housing
shortage; since entire neighbourhoods were suddenly zoned for single-

family use only, it both rendered the existing rooming houses illegal, and prevented homeowners from converting their dwellings into multi-family units.

"This growing movement toward Vancouver has been felt markedly during the past 10 months, several cartage companies in the city reporting increases in the Vancouver-bound traffic," reported the *Vancouver Sun*. "A direct result of the inflow of new residents has been the heavy demands for rentals for modern houses. There is a distinct shortage of this type of house, real estate men report, and soon scarcely any will be available."

By the time Gutteridge took office in 1937, Vancouver was horrendously overcrowded. The vacancy rate for houses sat at one per cent. Apartment suites, at two per cent, were scarcely better. And a disproportionate amount of this rental housing was in terrible shape. Most of the city's roughly eighteen hundred licensed rooming houses were stuffed well beyond capacity, in one case — at 1301 Robson — housing up to nine people in a single basement suite, with only one toilet, and without adequate light or ventilation. In the East End, inspector's reports described rotten floors, leaking roofs, rat infestations, and children sleeping in bathtubs. Tenants unable to pay up were often subject to immediate eviction at the hands of the city sheriff, their belongings unceremoniously tossed into the street. The shacks on the foreshore of False Creek and Burrard Inlet were now home to at least three hundred people — homes without electricity, running water, or sewage. And for the approximately thirty per cent of the male population then unemployed, there were few options other than the "hobo jungles."

As early as the summer of 1931, hobo jungles — large, open-air camps set up on vacant city properties — had sprung up across town, housing over one thousand people; by September, a camp at the corner of Prior and Campbell Streets was home to 450 men. Another, beneath the Georgia viaduct, was home to another 250 — all of whom shared a single toilet. Despite their hardships, unemployed workers received little sympathy from any level of government; originally a federal and provincial government responsibility, unemployment relief had been handed off to civic governments in 1932, but the cities had neither the staff nor the budget to make any meaningful difference. It was these squalid conditions and the ongoing, widespread unemployment which had led to the birth of the CCF in the first place. Formed in Alberta in August of 1932, the Vancouver arm of the CCF was represented by a group of powerful, socialist-minded women — most of them raised or educated in England. Cofounder Agnes Macphail was Canada's first female MP, and Dorothy Steeves went on to become a CCF MLA in North Vancouver. MP Frances Moren opened a free birth control clinic for young women — the first in Vancouver, and the second in the entire country. Owing to widespread economic unrest, interest in socialism had been on the rise in cities across Canada, and by the provincial election of 1935, seven CCF candidates were elected to the legislature, forming the official opposition against Premier Thomas Dufferin "Duff" Pattullo. Vancouver even had its own socialist radio station (operated by Moren's partner and future mayor Lyle Telford). And while not officially a party at the civic level, the CCF nonetheless sponsored candidates throughout the 1930s — including Helena Gutteridge. She was a perfect fit for the party. Tenacious and unafraid of conflict, she had scandalized her peers at the age of forty by marrying a man fifteen years her junior — and then leaving him after discovering he had been having an affair. One year before her election, she had descended on city hall to personally confront mayor George C. Miller, on behalf of the city's unemployed.

"I suppose, madam, you could tell us how to run the city?" Miller had sputtered.

Gutteridge smiled. "I have no doubt, sir, that I could."

Within a few months of her election, Gutteridge was on seven standing committees, and chairing an eighth. And before the year was out, she would become the de facto face of the city's accommodation crisis, when she formed — and chaired — the Special Committee On Housing.

Comprised of Gutteridge, Frank Buck (Chairman of the Town Planning Commission), and Albert Harrison (Secretary of Zoning), the committee's goals were to collect data on substandard living conditions citywide, and ultimately present a development plan to council. The team spent much of the spring and summer of 1937 knocking on doors in the West End, delivering an interim report in the fall, before proceeding on to the waterfront shacks and hobo jungles. Together, they filed several other reports throughout 1938 and 1939, and the details were positively Dickensian.

"When the tide is out they settle into mud, slime and filthy water," Buck wrote, of the False Creek float houses. "Water full of drifting waste and fouled with human excrement. One area reeks with the stench of decaying things, another with the gases arising from the fountain-like discharge from a sewage outlet just beyond the shacks, a fountain of continuous pollution, and of eternal shame so long as it poisons the waters on which float the huts of human beings." Children, he continued, "are held in dark basement suites fit only for storage, as if they themselves were but storage materials and not potential citizens who tomorrow must play some part in our civilization."

"Relative to the matter of shacks built along the foreshore at different locations after conference with the Chief Sanitary Inspector, I am of the opinion that the majority of the occupants are not there by choice," a January 1938 report added. "The lack of suitable housing at a rental which the occupants could afford to pay seems to be the main reason for the increasing number using this class of shelter."

Distraught, Gutteridge and Buck wrote to the federal government after filing their interim report in the fall of 1937, pleading for funds to help alleviate the housing crisis. They were rebuffed. Undeterred, the committee drafted and tabled a civic "standard of housing" bylaw, requiring that all city buildings be sanitary, well-ventilated, and in a state of good repair. In the meantime, Gutteridge made speeches and held rallies, working with the newly-formed Vancouver Housing Association on an educational campaign that pushed for a subsidized housing program. At her urging, sixteen civic and charitable organizations spoke at a meeting of the Building, Civic Parks, and Planning Committee (which Gutteridge chaired). When, in the summer of 1938, a fire in a building deemed unfit for human occupation claimed the lives of three children, Gutteridge strenuously resisted the widespread calls for demolition.

"We cannot condemn these buildings, because there are no other places for people to go," she told the *Daily Province*. "We need a low-rental housing scheme that will provide plenty of houses, to be let at whatever rental a low-wage earner can afford to pay."

Unfortunately for Gutteridge, social housing was an unfamiliar concept in Canada in the 1930s and 1940s. Instead, the federal government of R.B. Bennett preferred to stimulate private enterprise through passage of the Dominion Housing Act. Like the BHS before it, the DHA did very little for the low-income earners it was intended to help, instead being a series of subsidies for the construction industry. But by that point, Gutteridge had developed a scheme of her own. Through her work with the Vancouver Housing Authority, she had formed a relationship with Peter Stratton, a wealthy Englishman with an eye for charitable endeavours (he had already developed a free animal clinic and a drop-in centre for family planning in Vancouver). Having grown up around the slums of London, Stratton was convinced to donate four acres of his own land near Trout Lake, upon which the VHA would build a subsidized housing project. At the time, interest was sufficient enough that Gutteridge had even secured a second bid from a limited-dividend company, Pacific Housing Corporation.

**Conditions in one of Vancouver's 'Hobo Jungles,' 1931.
Image courtesy of CVA. Photo by W.J. Moore.**

But just like with the BHS of 1919, council wouldn't hear of it.

According to the provisions of the Borden government's new Dominion Housing Act, a city couldn't levy taxes on any social housing project that amounted to more than one per cent of its construction costs — well below the taxes paid by the owners of nearby single-family homes. The vote on the project was a bitter one, with only Gutteridge and mayor (and fellow socialist) Lyle Telford in favour.

Then, at the end of 1939, Helena Rose Gutteridge lost her council seat. More insulting still, she was defeated by Henry Corey, who also subsequently took her place on the Town Planning Commission. Although by this time she had reportedly become disillusioned with city government, Gutteridge ran in 1940, and again in 1941 — both times making housing her primary issue.

"Some of the worst of these houses are offered for rent by some of our very prominent citizens," she told the *Vancouver Sun* in 1940. "These people will resist any attempt to force them into making repairs. I admit the property owners are getting a rough deal now, but they have made their money out of those old houses in the past — have, in fact, paid themselves back on their investment over and over again."

With the outbreak of World War II, opinions and times had changed. Gutteridge never again won a council seat, finishing near the bottom of the ballot in both 1940 and 1941. And as the war years proceeded, her standard of housing bylaw threatened to slip through the cracks.

"This is not a new condition," Gutteridge fumed in the pages of the paper, "and is not a surprise to persons and groups that have been endeavouring to get some action thereon for some time [. . .]. What has happened to the Standard of Housing bylaw reposing on the table at the City Hall for the past 18 months? Has Alderman Corey forgotten it?"

"We received a great deal of opposition in the city and the other members of the council thought that the time was inopportune while the nation was at war," Corey protested. "In the meantime, I thought that there was no possibility of the thing being passed and it was left in abeyance because there was neither public nor council demand for it."

But there was a very specific reason that council wasn't interested, and it had very little to do with the war. Following the rise of the CCF in the early 1930s, the province's business elite — many real estate professionals among them — were terrified. Simply put, a socialist government would be committed to the interests of working-class voters above those of the business community, and, fearing the effect a communist takeover might have on their profits, the province's top financiers and business owners convened the Kidd Commission in

1932, looking for ways to combat the CCF's growing influence. Their solution was pure politics; the commission opted to frame their effort as a "non-partisan" approach to government, framing political influence — in this case, the CCF's — as an impediment to their true goal: growth. And while the original commission was provincial in scope, certain BC businesspeople, including millionaire former Mayor W.H. Malkin, Victor Odlum, and Crown Life Insurance head Brenton Brown (all members of the city's business elite), decided to try that same approach at the civic level.

"Believing that party politics are subversive of good civic government," read a full-page ad in the *Vancouver Sun*, "the Vancouver Non-Partisan Association opposes the entry of any political party in the field of civic elections. This action is based on the conviction that the interests of Vancouver are not identical with the interests of any political party, and that the plain every-day needs of our city such as roads, sewers, schools, parks, fire and police protection should not be made the vehicle for selfish political advancement."

Once NPA candidates began to gain civic power, their first major act was one of selfish political advancement. In 1936, they spearheaded a successful referendum to abolish the city's traditional "ward system." This gave them an enormous competitive advantage at election time; while working-class candidates could generally scrape together enough funds to campaign in a single ward, they often lacked the capital for the large, citywide campaigns required under the new "at-large" system. More than any other, this decision assured the party's dominance at the civic level for the next forty years, during which time aldermen no longer hailed from all over the city, but instead came almost entirely from the posh west side. Consequently the special committee's report, and the standard of housing bylaw it engendered, were forgotten. Dismayed, Helena Gutteridge chose not to run for civic office in 1942. She spent the war years in Lemon Creek, as a welfare worker attending to the rights of the interned Japanese-Canadian population. And when she returned to Vancouver in 1947, it was once again as an advocate for low-income housing, giving a series of lectures entitled "Housing — a Social Responsibility."

The CCF itself fell apart amidst the anti-communist hysteria that swept North America during the late 1940s and early 1950s, but Gutteridge stayed engaged, adamantly refusing to grow old in the manner that society demanded. She joined a women's organization devoted to world peace and nuclear disarmament. She fought back against red-baiters, and worked diligently to delineate the difference between communists, and the democratic socialism she had always championed.

"I try always to follow the advice I give to other women," she explained, in a 1957 interview. "Take an interest in public affairs. Keep yourself informed and express your opinions. Above all, be active."

"No council member has been more faithful or more zealous than she," noted the *Daily Province*, upon her initial aldermanic defeat. "Had the other members of council evinced half her interest in this problem, Vancouver might, long since, have made some progress in satisfying the need for low-rent housing."

It would be many more years before Gutteridge's ideas, and those of the Special Committee on Housing, would achieve any traction. But in the 1950s, two public housing projects — Little Mountain in Mount Pleasant, and Orchard Park on Nanaimo Street — would be completed, guided by the hand of none other than Peter Stratton. Neither Gutteridge, nor Frank Buck would live to see it. Like his committee partner, Buck looked back on the 1939 report with a combination of frustration and sadness.

"My last report on housing," he lamented, in 1942, "like the autumn leaves on which I gaze at the moment, drifted like one of those leaves into some dark nook where it will be swept into the limbo of discarded things."

10.
EMPTY

"It is reported that owners of homes, anxious to sell at present boom prices, get the tenants out and then keep the houses vacant until they can make a sale. People are reluctant to buy homes which are rented, due to the difficulty in getting the tenants out. In Victoria, there are comparatively few houses being held vacant for sale. In Vancouver, however, there are believed to be quite a number."

— *Vancouver Sun*, September 21, 1944

AS CITY COUNCIL, the province, and the federal government waffled, the housing shortage grew steadily worse. Between 1938 and 1942, Vancouver's population grew by thirty thousand, but the number of houses built was fewer than seven thousand. By 1942, the vacancy rate for all dwellings stood at 1.22%, but for single-family homes — still the predominant form of shelter in the city — it was a paltry 0.78%.

Reports abounded of people sleeping in garages, or camping in Stanley Park. In October of 1942, city Building Inspector Andrew Haggart went before council, and warned that Vancouver was facing the "greatest shortage of dwelling accommodation in its history, and unless a housing scheme is evolved the unprecedented overcrowding of homes, apartments, and rooming houses will become steadily worse."

"In my 22 years of service with the city," he continued, "I have never found such conditions of overcrowding as prevail today. Tenants are often obliged to accept these conditions because no other places are available, and will even concur in evasion of regulations by landlords rather than face the prospect of having to obtain new quarters."

But in the meantime, hundreds of mansions in Shaughnessy stood vacant.

Thanks to provisions of the Shaughnessy Heights Restriction Act of 1911, multi-family dwellings were strictly forbidden — something the neighbourhood's wealthy white residents had enacted to keep it free from both low-income and Chinese-Canadian residents. As a result of the dwindling housing supply, prices increased, making them a hot commodity for speculators, and consequently, instead of bothering with tenants, Shaughnessy homebuyers instead opted to evict them, and leave their homes empty in anticipation of a quick sale (a *Vancouver Sun* estimate in late 1944 put the number at more than two hundred).

"There is also the question of houses being held vacant while awaiting sale," wrote the *Sun*. "In some cases the owners have ousted previous tenants on the grounds that they, the owners, required them for personal residence; then there is a change of mind and the owner holds the property vacant with a 'For Sale' sign attached."

Vancouver's rich, as it turned out, had weathered the Depression rather well. In fact, wealthy Vancouverites had used the abrupt drop in labour and material costs to their advantage, having large mansions constructed in Shaughnessy and along Marine Drive. George

Reifel, a wealthy liquor manufacturer and bootlegger, had his Casa Mia estate built in 1932, and paid the contractors entirely in cash — in one cartoonish display of excess, even paying architect Ross Lort with a one-thousand-dollar bill. But by the end of 1944, the housing crisis was about to land right in their backyard. The shortage had dominated the local newspapers for the better part of the year, by which point it was clear that some government intervention was inevitable. At the civic level, Mayor Jonathan Cornett proposed relaxing the Shaughnessy Restriction Act, in hopes that multi-family conversions might help to relieve the problem. Shaughnessy property owners went ballistic; represented in council by Alderman Henry Corey (a resident of West Point Grey and former nemesis of Helena Gutteridge), they threatened injunctions against anyone meddling with the neighbourhood, and warned that any construction or plumbing companies involved in illegal conversions would have their business licenses revoked. Around the same time, property owners even had the gall to push for reduced property taxes, arguing that wartime belt-tightening had brought down their property values. But they could only resist for so long. In the interim, the building department, at Andrew Haggart's direction, had begun quietly helping interested property owners circumvent zoning regulations. The Vancouver Labour Council sent delegations to city hall, and even began staging protests in front of homes where people were being evicted.

But at the end of 1944, the matter was taken out of the city's hands altogether.

Coming into effect in the summer of 1945, the National Housing Registry was Ottawa's most direct intervention in the market to date. Spearheaded by Attorney General R.L. Maitland, it required every homeowner in the country to register vacant suites and dwellings, and levied severe penalties for non-compliance. In Vancouver, the program was overseen by former air Vice-Marshall Leigh Stevenson, and his first task was to verify the number of empty homes still available.

"The bona fides of every vacant house in the city are to be inquired into," the *Sun* noted, "the new policy is that it will not be allowed to be vacant long."

Yet again, city hall resisted.

"Why should a piece of empty real estate be sacrosanct?" complained the *Sun*, in an editorial chastising council for its stated desire to push back against Ottawa. "Is the owner's right to keep it vacant superior to the right of local families to have a roof over their heads? Any public representative who answers 'yes' to that question is not only out of sympathy with humanity but out of step with social progress."

But by the fall, Stevenson's report wasn't particularly encouraging. Of the roughly one hundred vacant houses that remained, at least half were either listed as "Unable to Contact Owner," or "Held For Sale," and thus unusable. In the end, the national housing registry, like the Dominion Housing Act before it, turned out to be just another empty promise. In the interim, organizations like the New Veterans floated other ideas to meet the city's housing needs, but ultimately, it was only their direct action at the Hotel Vancouver that pushed governments into action. And as the 1940s drew to a close, with population growing, and density constantly increasing, civic planning had become far too complex for the ostensibly part-time council and its standing committees to handle. This in turn led to the ascendancy of a man who would rapidly become the most powerful person at city hall — more powerful than council and even the mayor.

His name was Gerald Sutton Brown, and for the next twenty years, he would be a lightning rod for controversy, someone whom developers loved and hated in turn, a man with the power to transform entire neighbourhoods — or destroy them.

11.

"HAUNT OF THE RAGGED"

*"Housing costs are high, but we can't afford to
throw up our hands and say we can't afford to
build many more houses until costs come down
again. In a city growing as fast as ours this
would be the counsel of stupidity and despair.
We must have more homes and we must have
them at prices people can afford to pay."*

— *Vancouver Sun*, 1958

IT WAS EARLY in October 1953 when a lean-faced, forty-one-year-
old Englishman took the podium at the Vancouver Rotary Club and
outlined his vision for the future.

"To show imagination is easy," he told the crowd, in a clipped,
British accent, "but to make the most imaginative use of limited
resources — that is where the planner's skill is fully tested."

Ensuring Vancouver's future prosperity, he argued, would be a matter
of "aggressive forward-looking policy," guided by experts at city hall.

"Any slackness or lack of forethought at this critical stage in Vancouver's planning," he added, "could prejudice the future," but "by an aggressive policy we can ensure prosperity progressively in each five-year period."

It had been less than a year since Gerald Sutton Brown was hired as Vancouver's first official city planner. Described by the *Sun* as a "man who adequately contains whatever deep emotions he feels behind a Rex Harrison mask of English urbanity, pinstripes, an unlit pipe, and prettily coloured booklets of plans," he exemplified the post-war attitude to urban development. The 1950s were the decade that saw the rise of city planning as a science, and from the moment he was hired, in mid-1952, the contemplative, pipe-smoking civil engineer spoke of development in scientific terms, stressing a need for growth, efficiency, and objectivity.

After the war ended, governments across Canada had begun to worry about how to keep the economy from returning to its Depression-era depths. Thanks to the proliferation of the automobile, cities faced rapid urbanization, as well as continued population growth and dispersement — problems which required an entirely new set of solutions. In most Canadian cities — Vancouver included — this led to the creation of dedicated planning departments, staffed by experts in the field. Prior to 1950, planning matters had been dealt with in a more or less ad hoc fashion by the Town Planning Commission, a body comprised of aldermen — most of whom were real estate professionals — who acted in an advisory capacity, but following the NPA's establishment of the Technical Planning Board in 1951, the city planner became an integral part of day-to-day civic life. Although he lived and worked in the city for roughly twenty years, Sutton Brown was never particularly enamoured of Vancouver, as evidenced by multiple newspaper interviews, and by the fact that, in an effort to woo him, council awarded him a salary well above what had been advertised.

In the beginning, the city's business elite was overjoyed. Throughout the late 1940s and early 1950s, much of Vancouver's development had taken place outside of the downtown core. After 5:00 p.m., the central business district became a ghost town, as commuters streamed outward to homes in the suburbs, where they were easily serviced by emerging shopping centres. As a result, downtown property values plummeted. In 1951, the Vancouver Board of Trade pleaded with council to intervene, and consequently, downtown revitalization became a major element of the NPA's agenda — in particular, schemes which would use public money to stimulate private development.

In this, Sutton Brown and city hall were aligned.

His twenty-year plan for the city included four major elements typical of the modernist principles popular at the time: freeway construction, comprehensive zoning, downtown redevelopment, and urban renewal.

"There are some who expect the planner to accomplish the spectacular," he noted. "Well, what usually happens, everybody gets excited and nothing is done, because the spectacular usually is impractical. Development consists of the sweat and brains of a large number of people."

But when he spoke of "urban renewal," what Sutton Brown actually meant was slum clearance.

A concept that first began gaining traction in the 1940s, slum clearance had become popular amongst the urban planners of the 1950s, and while Vancouver's inner-city areas were nowhere near as bad as those in larger cities like London or New York, the media regularly decried the state of areas such as the Downtown East Side (then known as "Skid Road"), linking the area's physical decay to the supposed moral decay of its inhabitants.

"The haunt of the ragged," wailed the Vancouver *Province*. "Any Vancouverite who treads its pathetic streets today — flanked by grimy buildings, frequented by men and women who have sunk so low they know no shame — can appreciate the proportions of the crime that this metropolitan city has permitted and, in fact, perpetuates and subsidizes. [...] The seat of some of the worst squalor and poverty in Canada, an unsound, unsanitary cauldron into which the city wastefully pours twice as much money as it receives from the area in tax revenue — which means, in effect, that Vancouver taxpayers are subsidizing and paying to maintain the Skid Road."

In November of 1952, the paper ran a series bemoaning the state of Skid Road entitled "Street of Lost Souls." Shortly afterward, *Macleans* did the same. These articles made no examination of the root causes of poverty, nor did they investigate the speculators and property owners allowing their buildings to fall apart, instead attributing Skid Road's problems to the prevailing Protestant notion of poverty as a moral failing.

"To [Skid Road] gravitates the person who is unable to muster more social assets and who has been caught in a spiral of ever-increasing dependency," read a city social service department report. "He is often a homeless man who has experienced years of social isolation and is inadequate in some aspect of his personality."

In an interview with the paper, a major in the Salvation Army posited that what the Skid Road "derelicts" really needed was "some sort of work plan or character building."

"[T]here is," he said, "a need for them to face reality and acquire some initiative."

The "reality" was, urban decay in the downtown core had less to do with the Skid Road "derelict," and more to do with American tax policy; throughout the 1950s, rich Americans, faced with an income tax rate of ninety-one per cent, were actively looking for ways to keep capital out of government hands. Luckily for them, tax loopholes on both sides of the border allowed US speculators to write off up to sixty per cent of any money invested in Canada, which led to investors (like the Rockefeller family) sitting on a massive amount of downtown property (to the tune of one hundred million per year), while avoiding any expenses like basic upkeep.

Strathcona wasn't any better.

So named by social work professor Leonard Marsh in a 1950 report (after W.C. Van Horne, as it turned out, who was also known as "Lord Strathcona"), the neighbourhood was home to predominantly low-income families — many of them ethnic minorities. Bordering on Chinatown and including Hogan's Alley, it was home to both a vibrant Black and Chinese-Canadian community, known for its late-night cuisine (of the kind found at the legendary Vie's Steakhouse) and jazz. Nonetheless, city hall viewed the area with disdain; many homes were vacant or falling apart, garbage wasn't regularly collected, and the streets were cleaned by spraying them down with a slick substance that smelled of creosote. As early as 1949, a UBC study had proposed the "modernization" of Strathcona through slum clearance, but it wasn't until the arrival of Gerald Sutton Brown that this idea began to be taken seriously. In the eyes of the planning department, Skid Road and Strathcona were areas that needed to be cleansed. To do it would require plebiscites, capital, and expropriation on a massive scale, demanding the demolition of hundreds of homes, and the removal of thousands of citizens. It would be a massive undertaking, requiring considerable civic power.

But power was something Sutton Brown was gaining by the day.

The NPA had established the city's Planning Department in 1950, followed one year later by the Technical Planning Board (a smaller committee chaired by Sutton Brown), but in 1956, both of these bodies were rendered essentially obsolete by the creation of the Board of Administration — a three-person committee composed of two city commissioners (one of them being Sutton Brown) and the mayor. But because for most aldermen, council was a part-time job, and the Vancouver Charter allowed for considerable delegation to senior bureaucrats, the BOA became a sort of shadow government, allowing for the concentration of civic power in the hands of two unelected officials. Upon its formation, the BOA replaced thirty-four aldermanic committees, and from that moment forward, they essentially ran the city. Holding their meetings in secret, the board took over all day-to-day civic operations, and decided what issues they would submit to council — who virtually always accepted their recommendations. The commissioners — John Oliver and Sutton Brown — split their duties fifty-fifty, with Oliver taking on electrical, civil defence, fire, and court duties, and Sutton Brown managing building, planning, the budget, and social services. Like in most North American cities, Vancouver's council was deferential to experts like Sutton Brown, and the outside consultants he regularly used. However, unbeknownst to them, these same consultants were being cherry-picked by the city planner to validate his own personal conclusions. In practical terms, this meant that, from 1956 until 1973, Gerald Sutton Brown decided what was being built in Vancouver — period. He had final say on rezoning, development permits, and even design. By the late 1950s, council's role had shifted from generating policy to merely endorsing it. By 1961, even the mayor was no longer involved in BOA business.

Upon hearing this news, the Vancouver Association of Ratepayers was aghast. And there were many at City Hall who were concerned about the suddenly undemocratic nature of civic government. But for the time being, Sutton Brown couldn't be stopped. In 1957, he commissioned the Vancouver Redevelopment Study, which, in keeping with his goals, identified six areas ripe for urban renewal. Two of those areas comprised much of "Skid Road." The rest were in Chinatown and Strathcona. In total, the first two phases of the study called for the clearance of roughly sixty acres of private property, and the displacement of more than three thousand people.

"[T]he collar of slum and blighted properties [...] to the south and in particular to the east," a 1956 planning department report read, would require "surgical methods of cutting out old buildings and rebuilding as part of a comprehensive scheme of redevelopment."

In February of 1958, city council wholeheartedly approved the project.

"We consider this as in the best interests of the district and the city as a whole," Sutton Brown told reporters in April of 1958, reassuring wary property owners that when their homes were expropriated, they would receive "full market value."

And while Sutton Brown consulted with multiple experts about the possibilities surrounding urban renewal, the one group he didn't consult with were the residents of the neighbourhood. And residents were furious.

"They must be rehoused under at least minimum conditions for a healthy and useful existence," he noted, in the pages of the Vancouver Redevelopment Study. "If they are allowed to spread into adjacent areas as rebuilding takes place, it will spread the loss of economic values to other parts of the city."

But Chinatown property owners, having already been pushed to the margins for generations, weren't willing to be pushed around any longer. At a public meeting in April of 1958, a delegation from the newly-formed three-hundred-member Chinatown Property Owners Association confronted city council and demanded an explanation. Council took a conciliatory approach to the protestors, assuring them that the study was only preliminary. Yet, slightly over a week later, they rezoned ninety acres in the neighbourhood and began plans for "Urban Renewal Project Number One."

In the beginning, work proceeded slowly. Above the protestations of residents, the 1957 study was followed by another in 1959. Entitled "Freeways and Rapid Transit," it eschewed Sutton Brown's disdain for the "spectacular" by adding to the slum clearance project a massive freeway that cut through Chinatown and ran along the waterfront — a plan which would be built upon in subsequent years, and which aimed to displace more than twenty-five thousand people.

"We have initiated slum clearance which is the best in Canada," Sutton Brown proudly told the *Sun* in December of 1959. "No, it's not off the paper yet, but the paperwork is nearly at an end."

Phase one of the plan was formally adopted in 1960, and by the summer of 1961, the city had begun to expropriate property and remove families. This process continued for six years, involved twenty-eight acres, and removed sixteen hundred people from their homes. Phase two, approved in 1963, cleared another twenty-nine acres and displaced more than seventeen hundred people. And despite Sutton Brown's assurances of "fair market value," property owners found that they were being offered anything but; at a time when East End houses were going for ten thousand dollars to fifteen thousand dollars, the city was offering between seven and eight thousand — far too little for residents to remain in the neighbourhood. For the bulk of the 1950s, Vancouver's planning matters had been treated as technical, rather than political issues, and experts like Sutton Brown were viewed with reverence by both citizens and by council.

But by the late 1960s, this had begun to change.

As early as 1961, opposition to the project, and the displacements it would cause, was growing — first among neighbourhood advocacy groups, and then spreading into the academic community. Sutton Brown had already aroused public anger after requesting a plebiscite on the freeway scheme — one which was roundly defeated. Undeterred, he had asked for a second — this time about replacing the aging Georgia viaduct. The second referendum was a success, at which point Sutton Brown revealed to the city (and to council) that the viaducts had actually been part of the overall freeway plan all along. Vancouverites were outraged.

In the meantime, the planning department had commissioned at least three additional studies, all of them building on the original

1959 report, and culminating in Sutton Brown's master plan: the 1967 Vancouver Transportation Study. Also known as "Project 200," it called for an eight-lane freeway through Chinatown and Strathcona, running along the waterfront, and culminating in a new downtown civic centre. It would require the removal of 23,600 residents (whom Sutton Brown labelled as "deportees"), as well as the demolition of eight schools, eight churches, three daycares, and a number of social clubs and SRO hotels. During a June 15 public meeting, city hall was packed with angry people. During his presentation, Project Manager Harry Quinby could barely be heard above a chorus of jeers. And while the original protestors had been mostly Chinatown merchants and residents, they had since been joined by academics and city officials who were publicly denouncing the project, including alderman Harry Rankin, and UBC academics Walter Hardwick and Setty Pendakur. To the surprise of council, freeways and slum clearance had grown into political issues, and in response to the backlash, several aldermen withdrew their public support. Several business organizations, including the Downtown Business Owners Association, followed suit. In the days that followed, it became increasingly clear that city council hadn't fully understood the scale of the project they had ratified. Its scope was outside civic jurisdiction, and the experts brought in to study the problem had been told by Sutton Brown to focus only on traffic flow, not on the social or environmental costs. In addition, citizens were furious about Sutton Brown's dictatorial style, and the secretive nature of a process that was set to displace so many people from their homes.

"We are therefore shocked and horrified that this decision has been made without reference to the community at large," wrote Moira Sweeny, chairman of the Community Arts Council, "the citizens directly affected, the public organizations which had previously shown deep interest in this subject, and perhaps most damning, the duly-appointed citizen advisers, the town planning commission. We question the feasibility of the structure itself, its impact on property investment downtown, and its social impact on the community at large."

Council's position was initially unsympathetic.

During a second meeting, held on July 5, the mayor and four NPA councillors walked out after listening to only half an hour of protests. They voted against calling a third meeting, until public pressure changed their mind. The third meeting, in November of 1967, was attended by more than five hundred people. Unfortunately, the city deliberately monopolized the proceedings by having their delegation give a three-hour presentation — at which point it descended into chaos, and had to be adjourned. In many ways, the city's position at the time was most reflective of the man who sat in the mayor's chair: Tom Campbell. A real estate magnate who owned more than five hundred suites citywide, Campbell had never met a development project he didn't like (he would later throw his support behind a mega-hotel at the entrance to Stanley Park that also attracted considerable public outrage). Arrogant, petty, and mean-spirited (he was known derisively as "Tom Terrific" by his many enemies), Campbell did everything he could during the hearing process to frustrate protestors and scuttle debate.

But by the end of 1967, the matter was taken out of his hands.

In October, federal Housing Minister Paul Hellyer arrived to survey the proposed urban renewal and freeway sites. He attended meetings, and heard from Project 200's many opponents. During his stay, protestors gathered beneath the window of his hotel room.

Shortly afterward, Hellyer declared that no federal funding would be made available for Project 200. Two weeks later, at a public meeting attended by more than eight hundred people, Dr. Peter Oberlander, chairman of the Town Planning Commission, resigned in protest, on the grounds that "decisions on freeways were being made before the people know what kind of city they want."

Between 1952 and 1972, a total of forty-five studies had been conducted on freeways in the Vancouver area. And yet, other than the Georgia and Dunsmuir viaducts (opening amidst a storm of protest in 1972), and the displacement of twenty-three hundred people, very little had been accomplished. As for Sutton Brown's Project 200 — it was officially dead by the end of 1968. The ad hoc nature of the planning process, lack of federal funding, and issues surrounding jurisdiction had left the scheme on shaky ground, allowing public pressure to deliver the final blow. Of course, this was little comfort to the "deportees" of Chinatown and Strathcona.

But while the eyes of the city were focused on Project 200, something else had shifted at the provincial level. At first glance, it seemed like a relatively benign piece of legislation, introduced in September of 1966 by Attorney General Robert Bonner. And in the beginning, few understood how powerful and transformative those few strokes of a pen would be.

It wasn't urban renewal exactly, but it was about to change the face of the city forever.

"CASTLES IN THE AIR"
(1966 – 1984)

"The current pattern of downtown development differs in scale from Vancouver's previous boom periods. Just about everything else is the same — immense profits for a few property speculators, both local and foreign-based, behind-the-scenes wheeling and dealing between property interests and political parties, and a city administration controlled by real estate interest actively aiding developers and speculators in their activities."

— Donald Gutstein, Vancouver Ltd, 1975

12.
STRATA-FIED

"The association suggests that land speculators, in their greed for quick capital gains and profits in bidding for land offered for tender by Cities and Municipalities, have raised the cost of serviced lots beyond all reason, far beyond the limits of scarcity."

— "A Brief On Housing,"
Vancouver Civic Action Committee, 1967

IN JUNE OF 1973, *Sun* columnist Allan Fotheringham reported on a "pitiful scene" unfolding in the lobby of West Vancouver's Crescent View apartment building.

"The elderly residents were having a meeting to see if they could do anything about the ultimatum proffered to them by their new landlord, Dawson Developments," he wrote. "Their suites are being converted to condominiums, all very legal, and they must buy them or get out."

That most of Crescent View's residents were on fixed incomes didn't seem to matter to Dawson Developments, nor did the fact that many of them were in their eighties. Half were widows, Fotheringham noted, and some were so frail, they had to be attended by day nurses.

"I'm the youngest guy in the whole building," a man in his early sixties said. "A year from now a lot of these tenants may not be alive. And they're being told to buy their suites."

"On Monday," Fotheringham continued, "during the worry entailed in old people being faced with a move, one elderly woman had a stroke."

But despite their outrage, and the resultant media coverage, there was very little that Crescent View's residents could do. They were hardly the first — and far from the last — to fall victim to the wave of condo conversions then sweeping the city, courtesy of developer greed and an eight-year-old piece of provincial legislation known as the Strata Titles Act.

Introduced in late 1966 by Attorney General Robert Bonner, the Act — taken from similar laws being introduced across the western world — was a progressive piece of legislation for its time; prior to its passage, BC's apartment buildings were considered a single piece of property — units within could be rented, but ownership of the building itself remained in the hands of a single individual. The Act allowed for the subdivision of a building into units for individual sale, with the intention of providing an affordable option for lower and middle-income earners, and alleviating the ongoing housing shortage that still plagued much of North America.

"Western man's stubborn desire to own his own little nest, even if it is suspended fifteen storeys in the air, has been given official recognition by the provincial government," noted the *Sun*, in a 1966 primer entitled "Castles in the Air." "The Strata Titles Act, introduced in the legislature by Mr Bonner, is designed to accommodate the newest phenomenon of vertical living, the condominium. In effect it makes property a three-dimensional proposition and puts apartment dwellers, for the first time, on an equal status with those who prefer to reside on the ground."

"Because it's new and untried here," the *Sun* warned, "mortgage lenders will take to it slowly."

But despite its progressive intentions, it wasn't long before the Act was being abused. Because subdivision applied to both new construction and existing buildings, the purchase and conversion of rental apartment towers suddenly provided developers with an unprecedented opportunity to make money.

One such developer was Jack Poole.

Tall and strapping, with a square jaw and thick eyebrows, Poole would cultivate a reputation as an aggressive businessman, and ultimately go on to become a real estate titan and political power-broker, intimately involved in the growth and development of late-twentieth-century Vancouver, a man spoken of in reverent tones by associates, and journalists like Peter C. Newman.

But in the late 1960s, he was, in his own words, "small potatoes."

Poole didn't come from money, but what he lacked in financial resources, he made up for in ingenuity; having grown up in rural Saskatchewan, he spent his youth on construction sites, and did a stint building modular homes before cold-calling Vancouver businessman Graham Dawson, and talking him into a business partnership. Dawson — whose father had constructed the Burrard Street Bridge — put up the money, and Poole took the helm.

In addition to modular homes, the newly-formed Dawson Developments became active in condominium construction, completing the province's first condo development project — Port Moody's Hi-View Estates — in 1968. In fact, one of Poole's earliest appearances in Vancouver media was a transparently self-serving quote on the merits of condo ownership in the pages of the *Sun*.

"The day of the reasonably-priced $18,000 house is past," he told the paper, "but the condominium will provide at least one answer to the housing crisis."

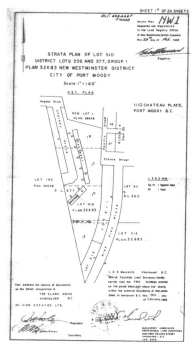

Plans for Hi-View Condominiums, BC's first condo development, 1968.

During the late 1960s, Vancouver's housing prices had soared; in 1967 alone, according to property assessments, the value of lots for single-family dwellings increased by more than twenty-five per cent — vastly outpacing the national market. At the same time, rental vacancy rates remained low; in 1965, more than six thousand new units had come online, yet the vacancy rate didn't waver. In 1958, seventy-five per cent of all housing starts were declared as single-family dwellings. But by the late 1960s, after the passage of the Strata Titles Act, apartment construction outnumbered house construction two-to-one. However, for developers like Dawson (soon renamed "Daon Developments"), the most profitable business strategy wasn't construction but displacement.

"Cash is everything in our business," Poole told the *Financial Post* in a 1974 interview. "That's the kind of strategy which will generate profit immediately and which will have us in a long cash position for 1974."

Before widespread changes to Canada's tax code in the early 1970s, apartment blocks were often the property of wealthy businesspeople, who used them as tax shelters. But with the 1971 tax overhaul came a sharp increase in condo conversions, as wealthy owners sought to offload their property — property which was eagerly snapped up and converted by developers. In 1971, the Metro Vancouver Land Registry Office registered seven conversion projects involving 119 rental units. By 1972, this figure had jumped to fourteen projects, and 305 units. Of course, it wasn't just Daon undertaking condo conversions; in that same year, according to the papers, at least fifteen other companies were involved, including the Capozzi Brothers, Link Developments, and Wall & Redekop, and the victims of displacement were often pensioners. But among its contemporaries, Daon was by far the most aggressive — by 1973, its revenues exceeded $43.8 million, and the company was able to quadruple its assets in just four years. By the mid-1970s, it was the second largest developer in North America. That these profits were often earned through practices that were — at best — unscrupulous and — at worst — predatory doesn't seem to have bothered Poole.

"Of course, in those days housing was so unrespectable," he later complained, to a *Sun* reporter. "I mean, it still is today. Very few people are prepared to admit that they have a friend who is a home builder or a developer. Developers are regarded as the lowest level of vermin in the world and that is unfair [...] The taller the building, the worse it is in the view of certain special interest groups — not the people who live in them. If you're not taking down a historical building you're taking down a church or you're encroaching on a park. Just everything you do is going to offend somebody ..."

In fact, it was often the people who lived in his buildings who were the most offended. In many cases, tenants were unable to afford to purchase their suites at the inflated prices demanded by their new landlords; in 1972, the conversion of the Aston Villa apartment block forced the eviction of two-thirds of its residents. The backlash from renters' rights groups was severe; one Link conversion project prompted widespread outrage after posting a sign outside the building which read "Less Than Rent!," prompting Link's General Manager P.F. Clarke to tell reporters: "Well, we don't mean that it costs less than what it does for the people who are renting in the building now. It means that it is less than renting in a more general sense."

The opposition continued throughout 1972. During this period, several city councillors and aldermanic hopefuls took up the cause — most of them from the left side of the political spectrum.

"In a city like Vancouver where reasonably-priced rental accommodation is very hard to get," argued NDP aldermanic candidate Amy Dalgleish, "it is shocking that elderly people with small incomes should be evicted from their homes for no other reason than the making of an exorbitant profit for a financial enterprise."

Bruce Yorke, secretary of the left-leaning Coalition of Progressive Electors (usually known as COPE) urged tenants to use small claims court to deter landlords, and NDP aldermanic candidate John Stanton took it even further, calling the behaviour of Daon and its contemporaries "very close to robbery."

During this period, opposition grew so vocal that Walter Harvey Link — head of Link Developments — publicly declared he was out of the conversion game altogether. In 1973, the newly-elected NDP government of Dave Barrett sought to help tenants by giving cities the ability to freeze condo conversions — something Vancouver City Council voted to do in June of the same year. North Vancouver quickly followed suit, and in 1974, the province overhauled the Strata Titles Act, making it necessary for owners to get civic approval before converting. While it did quiet some of the protest against the conversion process, it did very little to slow it; between 1979 and 1988, successive developer-friendly city councils approved seventy-five per cent of the rental conversion requests brought before them.

In the decade ahead, Daon Developments would continue to employ the same strategy, with the company overseeing tens of thousands of condominium conversions across the United States and Canada. At its peak, Daon employed nine hundred people, and occupied seven floors in a building they dubbed the "Golden Tower." Poole himself amassed a fortune, including a $2-million dollar mansion in West Vancouver, a private jet, and a retreat property in Idaho.

The elderly residents of Crescent View Apartments weren't quite so lucky.

Thanks to their inside connections at city hall, Daon managed to file the conversion paperwork for the building less than twenty-four hours before the deadline.

13.

THERE'S NO "I" IN "TEAM"

"[The government] believes that all people have the right to expect decent living accommodation. It believes that appropriate steps must be taken to assure an adequate supply of housing... not just to meet present needs, but to meet the needs of the future as well. A great deal of time has been spent, by both public and private authorities, on analyzing the housing problem. We must now concentrate our efforts on finding the solution."

— "Housing: Everyone's Responsibility,"
Department of Municipal Affairs, Victoria, 1969

IN JANUARY of 1973, after two tumultuous decades, Gerald Sutton Brown's career in Vancouver came to an end.

"At a secret meeting in Mayor Phillips' office at which Mr. Sutton

Brown was not present, the mayor and five new aldermen with no experience of the commissioner's work voted to retire an outstanding civic official with nearly 21 years of brilliant service behind him," fumed the Vancouver *Province*, in its editorial section. "So much for the techniques of sudden retirement."

While the paper decried it as a "guillotine job," Sutton Brown's abrupt resignation (shortly before he was due to be forcibly retired) signalled a change of direction in civic politics. In the years immediately following the Chinatown freeway debates, public opposition to large-scale development projects was more vociferous than ever. The opening of the Georgia and Dunsmuir viaducts, as well as the proposed demolition and redevelopment of Christchurch Cathedral, and a potential Four Seasons Hotel at the entrance to Stanley Park provoked widespread protest (egged on by the antagonistic attitude of Mayor Tom Campbell), and after forty years in power, the NPA's influence was fading. To fill the resulting power vacuum, two new parties emerged — both touting snazzy acronyms, and espousing a reform agenda: COPE and TEAM. COPE (the Coalition of Progressive Electors) was left-leaning; cast in the mold of the long-defunct CCF, they featured among their aldermanic candidates an actual communist (lawyer Harry Rankin). TEAM (The Electors Action Movement) branded themselves as a centrist party — one with a fresh outlook, and a set of friendly faces, including millionaire investor Art Phillips, and UBC academics Setty Pendakur and Walter Hardwick (both of whom had risen to civic prominence as vocal opponents of Sutton Brown's freeway plan). Following the election of 1972, TEAM went on to dominate city council; with Philips as mayor, councillors then implemented a series of notable changes at city hall, intended to make the planning process more transparent. The old BOA and Technical Planning Board were abolished, and replaced with a manager's advisory committee, chaired by the newly-created city manager. Local area planning was instituted. The mayor's job became full-time, and council meetings were moved into the evening, so they could be attended by interested members of the public.

But when it came to development itself, TEAM's goals and outlook were more or less identical to those of the NPA, as evidenced by the fluidity with which candidates and insiders switched back and forth between the two parties. Despite public protests that TEAM were "puppets" and "communists" by NPA Executive Secretary Brian Calder, both Mayor Art Phillips' assistant (a young property developer named Gordon Campbell) and Calder himself would ally themselves with both parties in the years to come. Calder in particular was something of a political Higgs-Boson particle (switching from the NPA to TEAM and then back again between 1968 and 1986), a man willing to take any position that furthered his own interests — and by the early 1970s, those interests meant property development. A businessman with a grade eleven education, Calder had been advocating for the development community in earnest since the election of 1966, when, as an aldermanic candidate, he had pushed a "total development plan" that included high-rise apartments in the downtown core, and windespread residential redevelopment. Then, after one term with the NPA, he switched to TEAM, at a time when the party was eyeing a development opportunity that Calder had been advocating for since the mid-1960s: the south shore of False Creek.

In the early part of the twentieth century, negotiations between the federal and provincial governments had resulted in the CPR being given control of the False Creek foreshore until 1970 — land they leased to a number of industrial tenants, including sawmills, shipyards, ironworks, and chemical plants. As a result, the False Creek basin had been the seat of Vancouver's heavy industry for decades, becoming progressively grimier and more polluted as the years passed, its water thick with the discharge from sixteen different sewage outfalls, and its air so thick with smoke, it would reportedly turn a white shirt grey. As early as 1929, the Harland Bartholomew Plan had called it "an eyesore and a menace to health," noting that "[i]ts regeneration is essential to normal civic development."

And things hadn't gotten much better in the ensuing years.

After the end of World War II, much of the industry surrounding False Creek moved outward in search of cheaper land, leaving an industrial wasteland in the centre of the city that lingered for decades.

Brian Calder, 1969.
(Image courtesy of CVA. Photo by Pugstem Publications.)

"False Creek means industry," reported the *Province*, in 1957. "It also means smog, a thousand smells, all bad, float houses, railways, boats and mud ... It is a monstrous thing of oily, wood-clogged waters, evil smelling homes. [It] is 'home' for the homeless, the down-and outers who sleep in alcoholic stupor on the railway-ribbed flats at the head of the creek. And it is a garbage dump, a sewer outlet, for the city of Vancouver."

But in the late 1960s, a series of land exchanges took place between the federal government, the province, and the city, with the city being the eventual recipient of 460 acres on the creek's south shore. During the Tom Campbell years, continued industrial use of False Creek was a foregone conclusion, but following TEAM's arrival on council in 1968, Phillips, Hardwick, and Calder began pushing an alternative concept — one which dovetailed nicely with the goals of the ever-expanding development community. Hardwick criticized Campbell's commitment to industry in the basin as an idea that was shaking the "confidence that Vancouver [was] a good place for investment," while Phillips took to the newspapers to explain the tax benefits that could come from rezoning the land, explaining to a *Sun* reporter in 1969 (in a phrase that could still serve as Vancouver's civic motto): "People are dying to go in there and build apartments."

"Nothing is more important in our future planning than preserving and improving the quality of life in our neighbourhoods," he added. "The waterfront should be a continuous system of parks and marinas for all the people to enjoy. False Creek will also provide housing for many people in an attractive setting. Young people and old people, families and singles and senior citizens should all be able to live in harmony with nature close to the downtown area."

Plans for development in False Creek had been ongoing in some form or another since at least 1968 (Gerald Sutton Brown had been involved in the early stages), but it wasn't until 1973, after TEAM gained control of council, that the plan could move ahead in earnest. A major step was to rezone the formerly industrial area — something which would not only allow for development on the south shore, but instantly increase the land value of the CPR's holdings (now owned by the railroad's development arm, Marathon Realty) on the north side of the basin from forty thousand dollars per acre to more than five hundred thousand. In hopes of capitalizing on the sudden jump in property values, a motion was introduced in council to demand fifty per cent of all proceeds from the rezoning. The vote was a close one, being narrowly defeated six to five, denying the city a significant financial windfall, and saving Marathon Realty a substantial amount of money (worth noting is the fact that shortly thereafter, Phillips' assistant Gordon Campbell left city hall to work for Marathon).

The False Creek project turned out to be startlingly progressive.

From 1970–1973, a series of planning groups had been working to determine the best use for the land, and an advisory committee (chaired by Hardwick and including Brian Calder) worked to determine the ideal mix of housing types, based on the actual incomes of Vancouverites in different economic brackets. Most significantly, the land was leased to developers by the city rather than sold outright, as part of a set of comprehensive land-use policies developed by TEAM (leading council to create the Property Endowment Fund in 1975; whereas the city had previously sold land to balance their budgets, the PEF allowed council to leverage their holdings for loans, balance their budgets, and generate a significant return on investment), and allowing the city much greater control of the project.

At first, resistance was substantial.

In February of 1974, False Creek Planning Committee member Craig Campbell resigned, charging that the entire process was "an outright scandal," and opining, in the pages of the *Sun*, that it was "among the very worst places in Vancouver on which to build a lot of housing." Other critics, including R.G. Raimondo of the Building Owners and Managers Association, warned that the mix of income-types would turn the region into a "slum area." Predictably, the Greater Vancouver Real Estate Board urged that construction begin as soon as possible, pushing the city to stop studying and start building. Complaints continued throughout 1974, from both within and outside of the planning department, including the viability of the project, and fears about mixing rich and poor. Nonetheless, construction began in 1976, spanning ten years, with the city being hands-on at every stage of the process, and in the end, the predicted slums never materialized. Ultimately, eighteen hundred dwellings were built — one-third of which were low-income rentals, one-third were co-op housing, and one-third were market condos (some leasehold and some freehold), sprinkled in between amenities like parkland, a school, a community centre, and winding, pedestrian-friendly streets. The land was provided on staggered sixty-year leases, with ground rents to be renegotiated every ten years. And offsetting the massive rezoning giveaway to Marathon, the city would be able to collect almost ten times as much in property taxes from new residential developments. In the end, the project was so successful that eight of the architects (and Mayor Phillips) moved in, and it has since come to be regarded as one of the most successful housing projects in Vancouver's history.

However, nearby Fairview Slopes didn't fare quite as well.

Owing to its proximity to the False Creek basin, it had always been a working-class district — a mix of students, families, artists, and blue-collar workers. However, with the redevelopment of False Creek, as surrounding land values rose, they were quickly replaced by residents with more education and fewer children. Rents, which in 1971 had been among the lowest in the city, jumped substantially over the next ten years, and by 1981, were actually higher than the citywide average. And naturally, speculators got in on the game; records show that the value of a single home on West 7th Avenue rose by 478% between 1969 and 1973. And after 1976, when the city rezoned the area to medium-density, this trend only accelerated. By the 1990s, more than half of the neighbourhood's pre-1976 housing stock had been torn down.

Outside of Fairview Slopes, conditions were becoming equally grim.

With redevelopment in vogue at city hall, and thanks to the financial possibilities provided by the Strata Titles Act, Vancouver's development community was now larger and stronger than ever; between 1961 and 1981, the city's finance, insurance, and real estate industries grew by a combined total of 207%. However, as had been the case for decades, a significant portion of those developers weren't local, and arguments about foreign ownership and global speculation quickly returned to the public discourse.

"Many downtown developers are foreign-controlled, and the majority of these, British in origin," wrote UBC academic Donald Gutstein in 1976. "Disregarding the hazy emotional arguments surrounding this situation, one point is crystal clear: by allowing foreign companies to buy our land, we are penalizing ourselves, driving up the price which we ourselves must pay. Allowing foreign ownership of downtown land means there are more buyers with money to spread, who are willing to pay much more than most Canadians can afford. With more potential buyers, the price of real estate automatically escalates, because the supply is limited — you cannot just create more land."

By 1975, one-third of the downtown core was owned by foreign companies — most of those from England. At the time, English money was frantically leaving a tight UK market, and flowing into the relatively stable, relatively unregulated world of Canadian real estate, and many, such as the Greater Vancouver Real Estate Board's Tom Boyle, didn't see much of a problem with the arrangement.

"If local buyers will pay me only $25,000 for my property," he retorted, "whereas I am offered twice as much by a British investor, then by not being allowed to sell to him, I have had half the value of my property expropriated."

At the same time, displacement and redevelopment weren't just the work of global corporations; locally-owned companies like Daon, Bentall, and Block Brothers remained major forces in the Canadian real estate scene throughout the 1970s. And even at the local level, some very ambitious players were quietly gearing up to reap huge profits in the redevelopment game.

They called themselves "The Town Group."

And their target was Vancouver's oldest neighbourhood.

14.

"LOCK, STOCK, AND CARRALL"

"Far too quickly Vancouver has reached a watershed in its short 90-year history. The choice is clear: to continue on the mindless drive toward a high-density prestige "executive city" — a Manhattan with mountains; or to redirect itself toward providing adequate housing and a decent environment for all classes of people. The first route is being promoted by those who currently control Vancouver's development. The second route will require drastic changes in the priorities of the decision-makers."

— Donald Gutstein, "Vancouver Ltd," 1976

GASTOWN WAS CRUMBLING.

By the mid-1960s, thanks to decades of owner neglect, it had become a dilapidated wasteland of vacant buildings, pockmarked asphalt, and grimy Single Room Occupancy (SRO) hotels — most built before the turn of the century. Windows were broken or boarded up, business was fleeing the area, and the sky was a spidery criss-cross of electrical wires. Like those profiled in the Vancouver *Province* during the 1950s, Gastown's residents were predominantly single men on meagre incomes. Many were Indigenous. Many were pensioners. Some of them had been there for decades, paying low rent (often around twenty dollars a month) to live in dingy single-room hotels like New Fountain, the Stanley, or the Rainier. More recently, they had been joined by a smattering of young hippies, drawn in by low rents, and recently displaced by police from Kitsilano's "acid row" (a series of run-down houses along 4th Avenue). Property values were abysmal, and as talk of Project 200 began to solidify, sales and development had slowed to a standstill, with banks unwilling to finance the purchase of any building likely to meet the wrecker's ball. Previous to this, a handful of merchants and activists had formed an organization called the Townsite Committee back in 1962, to champion Gastown's heritage, and push for a comprehensive restoration of the neighbourhood. Working with building owners, the Gastown Merchants' Association, and a nonprofit known as the Community Arts Council, the Townsite Committee commissioned a series of revitalization studies throughout the late 1960s, and in 1969, began hosting walking tours to raise awareness of the region's unique history and architecture. The Townsite Committee also worked with merchants to help beautify the exteriors of their buildings, in conjunction with academics from the UBC School of Architecture. But while their work had brought the preservation of Gastown into the public discourse, it had done little to spur any meaningful action from the city, the province, or the federal government.

Into this walked Larry Killam.

Inside of four years, the then-thirty-year-old developer would be celebrated by the media as the "spark-plug" of Gastown, credited with singlehandedly transforming the decaying neighbourhood into a hipster's paradise.

"Now it swings as no other in Canada but Vieux Montreal," wrote *Maclean's* magazine, in January of 1971. "Private enterprise rather than city planning affected the change, and one man — again — started it all."

In reality, the transformation of Gastown was hardly the work of a single individual. Rather, it was the result of years of dedicated work by the CAC, the Gastown Merchants' Association (and their president Stuart Keate), and Killam's partners — property magnates Howard Meakin and Bob Saunders, who first saw the area's potential. But for Killam, fresh from his first housing project in Toronto's Yorkville neighbourhood, heritage preservation was the last thing on his mind.

"Vancouver's skid road, he thought, was more interesting territory than the middle-class Yorkville environs," *Maclean's* noted. "There was no romance in his thinking. He was out to make money."

If there was one thing Killam knew, it was money. After all, he'd come from plenty of it.

Growing up in a wealthy Kerrisdale family, he had spent afternoons at the Vancouver Yacht Club, and summers holidaying in the British Isles, and after graduating from UBC, had tried his hand at a number of business ventures, including advertising and real estate. Contrary to newspaper profiles at the time, Killam wasn't the brainchild behind Gastown's revitalization; he had initially been approached by Meakin and Saunders, and the trio — along with several others — formed The Town Group, and spent much of the late 1960s buying up as much neighbourhood real estate as possible. Because no bank at the time would finance the purchase of Gastown property, it was necessary to buy the buildings outright — so like the Coal Harbour Syndicate before them, they brought in some partners. Killam's involvement may seem unusual, given his relative inexperience in development, but his knack for publicity and ready access to money (much of the cash for those initial purchases was borrowed from wealthy relatives) made him an indispensable part of the Town Group's operations.

"Killam's pursuit of creativity in 1969 has become one of the most lucrative financial ventures in Vancouver's history," wrote reporter Gary Bannerman, in a fawning profile in the *Vancouver Province*. "Since 1969, Killam and his colleagues have invested about $170,000. Escalating property values have given Town Group Ltd a $700,000 equity in $1.5 million of holdings."

The Town Group's first purchase was a building at 1 West Cordova — bought for a mere nineteen thousand dollars in the fall of 1966 (well below its asking price of forty-seven thousand dollars). Shortly thereafter, they got their hands on the decaying Alhambra Hotel, the oldest still-standing building in Gastown, and set about turning both into loft suites for young professionals. But as Gastown's newest landowners realized, their property values would only see a significant increase if the neighbourhood itself were visibly improved. This meant two things: public money, and the removal of Gastown's low-income population. To that end, property owners — including the Town Group — paid for a series of revitalization and beautification studies aimed at remaking the area as a heritage neighbourhood and boutique shopping district. In their 1969 report, consultants Birmingham and Wood recommended a number of aesthetic flourishes, including cobblestone streets, antique light standards, the burial of BC Hydro electrical wires, and the purchase of Blood and Trounce Alleys for a public square. Additionally, they advocated for the demolition of the Stanley and New Fountain hotels — both of which were falling apart — and "minimizing contact between the shopper and the destitute" via increased policing of the "offending population."

Led by Killam, a committee of Gastown merchants presented their plan to city council in mid-1971. Civic and provincial money, they argued, would lead to a widespread rise in Gastown property values (and thus, property tax revenues), which would be supplemented by provincial funds already pledged by MLA Herb Capozzi (for the burial of BC Hydro's electrical wires), and an additional local improvement tax paid by merchants themselves. The initial stage of the project would involve the creation of Maple Tree Square, a public gathering place designed by the Town Group's Bud Korvacs which would be constructed just outside the renovated Alhambra Hotel. The Town Group, and another Gillam-helmed organization called The Townsite Commission, would ultimately be responsible for all of the amenities in the neighbourhood, including the Gastown Steam Clock, and the Gassy Jack statue (designed by Korvacs, and donated to the city by Gillam in 1970 as a Valentine's Day present).

However, not everyone at city hall was initially enamoured by the neighbourhood's new direction.

"I asked him: 'How do you like our statue?'" Killam later recalled, of a conversation with then-Mayor Tom Campbell. "The Mayor looked at me and said: 'I've just instructed municipal works to remove that crock ... and place it in the dump.' Well, I knew he hadn't had time to see it properly so I turned to his wife and suggested she take Tom around that evening to look at it before going home. I didn't hear another word."

Nonetheless, council adopted the report, and set about putting its recommendations into motion. But for Killam and his partners at the Town Group, the transformation had already begun. By 1971, when the neighbourhood was said to be swinging "as no other in Canada but Vieux Montreal," the company had already converted several of their properties — including the Alhambra — into loft

suites for young professionals. The Town Group ultimately purchased ten buildings in the area, and inside of five years, their
property values had doubled, tripled, or more — 1 West Cordova,
originally purchased for nineteen thousand dollars, was suddenly
worth $125,000. And while these changes were a financial windfall
for Killam and his partners, their gain came at a substantial cost for
neighbourhood residents.

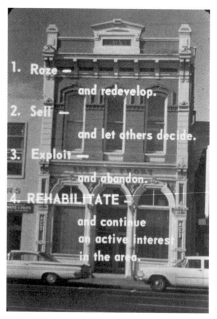

Gastown circa 1966. From a slide accompanying "The Townsite Story:
The Origins of Vancouver's Gastown Revitalization" written by
Melville Gerald Thomson. Image courtesy of CVA.

"Killam's invariable strategy was to kick out the derelicts and scrape away dirt and plaster to expose original beams and brick," *Maclean's* noted. "He would rent the rooms to a new kind of young people he had noticed in the area."

"We want no part in our buildings of the old alcoholic or the old-age pensioner, I'm sorry to say," Killam shrugged, in a 1970 interview with *The Province*.

"The sad thing is the old men who live there now," he added, of another building project. "None of them are alcoholics and many of them have been living there for 20 years or more at rents like $20 a month. They are going to have trouble finding accommodation at similar cost."

"And that, surely, is the understatement of the year!" retorted Vancouverite Patricia Kelly in a letter to the editor several days later. "What are they going to do? What will this and similar projects undertaken in Vancouver do to these people's whole world? [...] By all means, let us take pride in our city and encourage every move that will enhance its attractiveness — but not at the cost of the necessities of life of many of its citizens."

Opposition to the Gastown displacements was a large part of the public discourse throughout the late 1960s and early 1970s, but this didn't seem to matter to Killam. In fact, the Town Group's strategy was to remake the neighbourhood socially as well as aesthetically, and that meant removing any and all perceived "undesirables" — which to Killam meant not just alcoholics and drug users, but also gay men and women.

"When his apartments in the Alhambra Hotel and the Boulder Building started to rent, Killam says he was regularly faced with requests from homosexuals for accommodation," wrote *The Province*. To control this, and the drug problem, the apartments are incorporated as residential clubs that give the proprietor greater control of who gets accommodation. Undesirables are not admitted into the club."

As the displacements continued into the mid-1970s, the work of rehousing Gastown's population fell to city social planning director Maurice Egan, who, according to *The Province*, "inherited the job of looking after the rubbies knocked into the streets in the wake of restoration projects by Killam and his cohorts."

Throughout the process, Killam's apparent lack of scruples wasn't ignored by the media, or by his peers.

"I must emphasize that I admire what The Town Group has done," wrote Gastown Merchants' Association head Stuart Keate, in the *Sun*, "but they've concentrated more on the physical assets of the ledger than they have on the goodwill end." (Keate would later go on to write that Killam's strategy was to buy up Gastown, "Lock, Stock, and Carrall").

"Larry Killam, 30, is a capitalist," added *The Province*'s Gary Bannerman. "Like any successful businessman, he has a feeling for money and how to make it."

In the pages of *Maclean's*, a colleague was considerably more blunt in his assessment of Killam's character: "Killam," he told the magazine, "doesn't mean to do good. He is a carnivore among the vegetarians."

But all of this public criticism didn't seem to bother Killam; if anything, it encouraged him to double down.

"Initially the city reacted to my moves with joy," he protested. "Now I have their social problems like an albatross around my neck. But my attitude is that, since the city doubled taxes on Gastown buildings in a single year, the derelict problem is theirs. They've got a chunk of my dough to pay for the solution."

In 1974, Heritage Canada awarded its top honour to the Maple Tree Square and Blood Alley projects, and in the years that followed, Water Street merchants began work on their own heritage beautification scheme — culminating in the installation of the Gastown steam clock in 1977. Despite an aggressive push by merchants (and a demolition application filed in 1969), both the Stanley and New Fountain hotels were saved as low-income housing, thanks to the timely intervention of UBC Architecture Professor Harold Kalman, who spearheaded efforts to purchase and renovate the one-hundred-plus-year-old structures.

As for Killam, much like those he had displaced, his days in the neighbourhood were numbered. After a series of personality clashes with other Town Group members, he departed abruptly in 1975 — the matter wound up in court, at which point it was revealed that Killam had only ever been a minority shareholder in the company. His brother Eugene, a Town Group partner until 1969, had also found himself in legal trouble, after buying one million dollars in stolen pearls smuggled in from the US.

Killam kept a much lower profile after the Gastown years, but when he did reemerge, it was rarely in a flattering light. During the mid-1970s, he found himself embroiled in a court case involving government employees and a land speculation scandal. In 1976, he made the papers when he bought and demolished Duart, the iconic Shaughnessy mansion once owned by timber baron H.R. MacMillan. In 1985, as one of the directors of the Shaughnessy Heights Property Association, he helped force the closure of a home for twenty-five mentally ill men.

Today, the Alhambra still stands on the edge of Maple Tree Square, across the courtyard from the Stanley and New Fountain hotels. The neighbourhood has since undergone several cycles of decay and renewal, but otherwise remains virtually identical to the Town Group's vision, more than forty years later.

But Gastown wasn't the only neighbourhood changing throughout the 1970s. Even with increased supply in the wake of the Strata Titles Act, the city's vacancy rate had yet to improve, and all over town, cash-and-space-strapped locals were forced to come up with their own solutions to Vancouver's ongoing housing crisis.

They would soon find themselves under fire from city councillors, police, and even their own neighbours.

15.

MONSTER HOUSES

"The inability of younger households to afford 'family type' accommodation in the City has been one of the spin-offs of rising house prices... Households in the lowest income category, 18% of all households, have about 4% of the total income, while those in the highest category, 23% of all households, have 47% of the total income. The obvious implication is that much of the purchasing power in the City, including the ability to pay for housing, is concentrated in a relatively small proportion of households."

**— "Understanding Vancouver's Housing,"
Planning Department, City of Vancouver, 1979**

LARRY CUDNEY hated architects.

In fact, he hated the entire architectural profession. For a time, years earlier, while still a young intern with a local firm, he had harboured dreams of becoming one himself, until a falling-out with the company prevented him from obtaining the certification he needed. Embittered, Cudney developed a lifelong contempt for the profession that had spurned him, and struck out on his own. Working as a draftsman from his cramped office on Main Street and 33rd Avenue, he designed single-family homes (the only buildings a draftsman could legally design), and his work was known for being simple and practical, containing few architectural flourishes (he once told his stepdaughter Elizabeth Murphy that he had no interest in designing "a big stupid house as a monument for someone's big stupid life"). Reflecting Cudney's thrifty nature (he reportedly wore a suit he had purchased for less than a dollar, which he celebrated by leaving the price tag on), they could also be built from relatively inexpensive materials.

But then, sometime in the mid/late-1960s, Cudney sat down and drafted the plans that would become his legacy. It came to be known as the "Vancouver Special", and for the next twenty years, it would be the most widely-discussed — and hated — type of housing in town.

The phrase "Vancouver Special" itself had been circulating since the mid-1960s, originally as a blanket term describing cheap, simple-looking houses, but by 1974, as they began to appear en masse throughout the east end, the label came to be applied exclusively to Cudney's creation. Characterized by their box-like structure, pitched roof, and brick or stucco ground-floor finish, Vancouver Specials quickly proved popular with the city's working families, thanks in part to their cheap construction (permit-ready plans could be bought from Cudney for less than a hundred dollars, and the houses themselves could be built for roughly half the price-per-square-foot of other homes of the day). But, despite being beloved by many lower-income homebuyers, they proved substantially less popular with everyone else.

"Those brash new houses with slightly pitched roofs and aluminum balconies (known in the trade as Vancouver Specials), which are now squeezed into lots where once a single house stood in a magnificent garden are here not just to stay, but to increase," complained the *Sun*, in 1978.

"But by the time the city takes action the house is built," added the paper's Judy Lindsay. "It is usually large, and has been shoehorned into a single-family-sized lot leaving a tiny garden."

Vancouver Specials, circa 1970s.

Although Cudney himself retired in 1976, his design continued to proliferate. Between 1965 and 1985, an estimated ten thousand Vancouver Specials were built, and by 1980, according to a Young Canada Works survey, eleven per cent of Hastings-Sunrise, and five per cent of Marpole were made up of Vancouver Specials. And as more and more were built, the backlash only grew. Neighbourhood organizations distributed leaflets and harassed building crews. City council attempted to stop the spread of Vancouver Specials west of

Main Street. Their rise was bemoaned in letters to the editor (a 1984 letter in the pages of the *Sun* went so far as to call them a "cancer"). In 1984, the Canada Mortgage and Housing Corporation and the Architectural Institute of BC even sponsored a contest to find replacements for the design. By the spring of 1984, the debate over Vancouver Specials had grown so heated that they were the subject of a newspaper series by the *Sun*'s Pete McMartin (who referred to them as "singularly ugly"). In October, McMartin and Alderman George Puil took a tour of various east side neighbourhoods, and in 1986, the city held a number of town hall meetings to discuss the issue. In the meantime, Vancouver Specials were blamed for a variety of social and economic ills — everything from destroying neighbourhoods to driving up property values.

"Right now, to buy a house in the city's east side, you have to have $20,000 in assets and a $20,000 income," wrote the *Sun*'s Mary McAlpine in 1978. "Most young people with children don't have that sort of money. The people who do are developers who tear down the house and put up Vancouver Specials — those two-storey houses now popping up all over town with flat or slightly pitched roofs and aluminum balconies. The developers sell them to young professionals or multi-generation families for $80,000. So most young families are fleeing the city. The school population in Vancouver dropped 8,500 between 1970 and 1975, and is still dropping."

"Street after street of bland stucco boxes, devoid of architecture, devoid of charm," the *Sun*'s Barbara Pettit wrote, in March of 1984. "The Vancouver Special is a symptom of a city trying to change within a zoning framework designed to protect the character of single-family neighbourhoods. Despite rezoning, neighbourhoods have changed — into row after row of Vancouver Specials."

Indeed, zoning did figure into the backlash against Vancouver Specials, as part of a debate that had been going on since the days of Helena Gutteridge; with an impressive two thousand square feet to work with, the homes were ideally set up to allow for secondary suites. As a response to the city's wartime housing shortage, secondary suites had begun to proliferate throughout the 1940s, and were actively encouraged by council. However, by the end of the decade, the city had done a stark about-face, declaring them illegal, eventually mounting a program in 1959 to eradicate them altogether. This was a crusade that would be taken up by successive councils, on and off, for decades. The initial campaign quickly ran out of steam when council realized the role that secondary suites could play in alleviating the housing crunch, and the city ostensibly decided to look the other way after 1961, opting instead to address the suites on a complaint-only basis. Secondary suites remained ostensibly illegal into the 1970s (multi-family dwellings in a single-family neighbourhood ran afoul of zoning bylaws), and the cause was sporadically taken up by zealous councillors, including Puil and a young NPA candidate named Gordon Campbell. As before, it went nowhere, and for good reason; with property values steadily rising, and interest rates at a crushing sixteen per cent, the rental income from secondary suites was often something working families were counting on to subsidize their mortgages. The argument went on and on. And then, in 1985, the city introduced a host of building code changes — including limits on floor-space ratios — aimed at ending the reign of the Vancouver Special altogether.

It worked.

But in the years that followed, attitudes — including city council, and the *Sun*'s McMartin — began to change. For many lower-income and immigrant families, council later recognized, the Vancouver Special, was their only chance for home ownership. In 1987, City Councillor Gordon Price even praised the architectural style as "a tradition of our cultural diversity," and "worthy of heritage preservation." And by the early 2000s, Cudney's legacy was being re-examined; many renovated Specials have since appeared in the pages of architectural magazines, and been featured on historical walking tours. In 2005, a renovated Vancouver Special was awarded the Lieutenant-Governor's Award for Innovation in Architecture.

Privately, Larry Cudney was said to have been proud of the disgust his brainchild had engendered.

"Creating a completely tasteless form of housing," stepdaughter Elizabeth Murphy later opined, "was his revenge on the architect profession with which he was in conflict."

But, even though the fight over the Vancouver Special effectively ended with the building code changes of 1985, bigger trouble had been brewing in the interim for the city's renters.

And it would prove to be one of the longest battles for housing justice in a generation.

16.

RENT CONTROL (Part I)

"[I]n the rental situation in this province there was a necessity upon the part of any government with a heart to step in and protect within its powers tenants who were suffering intolerable pressures as a result of the plummeting vacancy rate, particularly in the lower mainland... When the chips are down and people are suffering unnecessary exploitation, and a great many tenants are suffering unnecessary exploitation at the present time, a government isn't worth its salt if it doesn't stand up and protect that class of people."

— Attorney General Alex MacDonald, April 8, 1974

IN JANUARY OF 1974, more than seven hundred people packed into the auditorium of Kitsilano High School to square off over the state of the city's rental market. Some were tenants. Many were landlords, or representatives from the city's major development companies, including Block Brothers Realty, and Wall & Redekop.

Tensions were running high.

Thanks to the profit potential unlocked by the Strata Titles Act, the global players in Vancouver's real estate market had basically abandoned rental apartments, and by 1974, the city's rental vacancy rate sat at an unprecedented 0.2%. To make things worse, the roughly fifty per cent of Vancouverites who rented had seen their monthly housing charges increase by ten to twenty per cent in 1973 alone. After years of public back-and-forth between renters and landlords (which had included rent strikes and legal action), spearheaded by the newly-formed Vancouver Tenants Union, the public meeting had been called by communist lawyer and alderman Harry Rankin, in an attempt to get a handle on the problem.

It didn't take long before it descended into chaos.

Attendees hurled insults, shouted one another down, and attempted to win council support for their respective causes — which, for the Tenants Union (established as an unofficial body just five years earlier), included a demand which had sent the real estate industry into an apoplectic fury: rent control.

This wasn't the first time the concept had been discussed; during World War II, in an attempt to combat the housing crunch, the province had established short-term rent controls, governed by the Wartime Price Board, which had set provincial rental rates, and levied fines against landlords for noncompliance. While the legislation was repealed following the war, rent control became a cause which was occasionally taken up by city councillors (including Harry Rankin and Halford Wilson) beginning in the 1960s. In late 1967, Vancouver-Burrard NDP MLA Tom Berger introduced a private member's bill in

Victoria pushing for a tenant's bill of rights, which included items such as a one-year freeze on rent increases, two months notice of eviction, and a one-month maximum on security deposits.

The bill went nowhere.

During the Tom Campbell years, Rankin put forward a motion for civic rent control, after discovering an obscure provision in the 1954 provincial Rent Control Act, which ostensibly granted the city the power to enact such measures without appealing to the province. This too was ignored. Through the majority of the 1960s, the city and the province took no meaningful action of any kind, choosing instead to quibble about jurisdiction. And the issue might have remained in limbo if it weren't for Bruce Yorke.

Then fifty-one, Yorke was a well-known social justice activist, and card-carrying member of the Communist Party. With greying hair and thick eyebrows, he had graduated from UBC with a bachelor's degree in economics, and was subsequently awarded a PhD scholarship to MIT, until his communist leanings led the American government to have him deported. A founding member of COPE, alongside Harry Rankin, Yorke subsequently devoted himself to a series of labour and left-wing causes, and then, in 1968, decided to form the Vancouver Tenants Council (later the Tenant's Union) to protect the rights of renters.

"In August, 1968, we held our first meeting of tenants," he later recalled. "It was at the Driftwood apartment in Kitsilano. I took the initiative in calling that meeting. The main issue disturbing tenants was a 5% increase in rents imposed on very short notice, plus a rather insulting letter from Block Brothers."

The meeting, held at Kitsilano Beach, was attended by at least seventy-five tenants from the Driftwood Apartments, and generated substantial media coverage.

"We didn't win that battle," Yorke added, "but we did establish the fact that tenants were determined to get organized and make their voices heard."

Throughout most of the twentieth century, tenants in BC have had very few rights; outside of small-claims court, they had no protection from evictions, rent increases, unfair security deposits, or hefty repair bills. Up until 1978, they also couldn't vote on civic expenditures (according to the Vancouver Charter, only property owners could vote on new capital projects). Yorke and the Tenants Union aimed to change that. And while the Driftwood campaign was unsuccessful, the group persisted, attracting new members in droves, and initiating a rent strike in the Rosemount Apartments on Broadway, to protest rate increases and unfair security deposits. While Yorke was organizing tenants, Rankin continued to push for rent control provisions in city council, and, in April of 1968, convened a committee to study the issue. The real estate industry began immediately frothing at the mouth. Mayor Campbell and several right-of-centre aldermen pushed to have the committee disbanded, and Councillor Ernie Broome took to the newspapers to complain.

"Council is opening up a Pandora's Box of ills," he protested. "This can cause a lot of harm to the city."

"We can police ourselves quite well," sputtered Bill Wallace, Secretary of the Vancouver Apartment and Lodging House Association, "and anyway, if tenants aren't happy they can always move out."

"Some of these [Tenants Union] leaders not only have socialist backgrounds, they also have Communist leanings," Vancouver Centre MLA Herb Capozzi warned, in a meeting with the Apartment and Rooming House Operators Association. "They are using their positions to try and break down the free-enterprise system that allows a man who takes a risk to reap some reward." (It should be noted that in addition to being an MLA, Capozzi himself was in the housing game — making the papers in the early 1970s for condo conversions that had evicted a number of lower-income tenants).

Despite the bluster, and in large part because of the VTU's actions at the Rosemount, council passed a bylaw in September of 1969 —

drawn up by Yoke and Rankin — that established a civic Rental Grievance Board, to provide some protection for local renters.

"These included a maximum of one rent increase per year," Yorke later wrote, "three months notice of rent increases (a by-product of our victory in Rosemount), a $25 limit on security deposits, landlord responsibility for repairs and mitigation of damages."

The committee would be neutered almost instantly. While it was initially comprised of just two aldermen and the mayor, Campbell (himself the owner of thousands of apartment units) subsequently introduced a motion requiring every city councillor to be present before a meeting could be held (and since most of them were against the idea, they simply didn't show up).

The debate over rent control continued into the early 1970s, at the civic, provincial, and federal level, and by 1970, the expanded BC Tenants Union represented more than three thousand people. As a result of numerous protest actions, the province's Landlord and Tenant Act was amended in 1970, to include many of the provisions Yorke and Rankin had demanded from the city: three months notice for eviction, once-annual rent increases, and the elimination of eviction without cause — a first in provincial history. In April of 1971, the union spearheaded a ten-month rent strike to protest the ten per cent increase in rents at a Wall & Redekop building.

"[A] landlord is entitled to a rate of return," Rankin told a town hall meeting in 1969, "but that you are entitled to have this explained in actual rise in cost of living costs. Is it right, proper or just for landlords to take advantage of the shortage of accommodation? There must be some kind of controls over the basic commodities of life, which include accommodation."

"So if we try to control rents, what's to prevent us from moving into other fields, like the price of clothing or food?" sputtered NPA alderman (and future developer) Brian Calder. (Unusually, price controls on food were an idea Calder had encouraged just one day earlier, quoted in the pages of the *Sun* as saying: "I would rather see us go after food prices which have risen much faster than rents, or clothing for kids.")

But then, in 1972, the NDP government of premier Dave Barrett took power.

Barrett, a former social worker and civil servant, had been the first provincial premier to make rent control part of his election platform, and once elected, began working toward updating the Landlord and Tenant Act as one of a series of worker-focused, regulatory reforms (the NDP also established the Insurance Corporation of British Columbia (ICBC), the Labour Relations Board, and the Agricultural Land Reserve). As the legislation was being redrafted, Barrett introduced the Interim Rent Stabilization Act in the spring of 1974, which capped annual rent increases at eight per cent. The real estate industry, and the opposition Social Credit government, were furious.

"I have called many of the developers in British Columbia who traditionally have looked after our supply of rental accommodations," grumbled Social Credit MLA Pat McGeer, during a debate in the legislature. "Every single one I have contacted has said they're going to put up no rental accommodation—not just decrease it, they're dropping it to zero."

"If anyone had come to me and said that socialists were this ignorant of economics," sneered MLA Harvey Schroeder, "and that they would add insult to injury by trying to correct a problem by stacking more problems on top of it, I would not have believed it."

"[I]n the rental situation in this province there was a necessity upon the part of any government with a heart to step in and protect within its powers tenants who were suffering intolerable pressures as a result of the plummeting vacancy rate, particularly in the Lower Mainland," replied Attorney General Alex MacDonald. "When the chips are down and people are suffering unnecessary exploitation, and a great many tenants are suffering unnecessary exploitation at the present time, a government isn't worth its salt if it doesn't stand up and protect that class of people."

"License is given to exploit," added MLA Emery Barnes. "Landlords take it as a basic right... it's about time there is a responsibility on the part of landlords to the people they serve. I think they [landlords] are going to have to be prepared to settle for a simple equity value rather than having extra benefits above and beyond that. [Rent control is] just a beginning ... as far as this government is concerned, in trying to straighten out some of the inequities within our society."

At the same time, starting in 1974, the province initiated a series of subsidy programs to stimulate the private development of rental properties, known by the awkward acronyms ARP and MURB (the Affordable Rental Program, and the Multiple Unit Residential Building Subsidy, respectively).

"Replace it [Interim Act] by one that offers incentives to the developer," Pat McGeer demanded. "You will have solved the problem in the only way that works — in the classic way — by providing supply."

It didn't work.

Like the Better Housing Scheme before it, ARP and MURB were simply abused by developers (including, notably, Daon Developments' Anchor Point project), to reap additional profits, while ultimately providing zero affordable housing. Even worse, most ARP projects were registered as strata, not rental, meaning they ostensibly also provided no additional supply for renters.

"ARP did everything for the investor but nail up the boards," wrote the *Sun*'s Linda Hosie, in a 1979 postmortem. "It provided up to $3000 a year in grants and interest-free loans [per unit]. Under the ARP subsidy rules higher costs bring higher returns. If the project fails and is sold at cost (and existing ARP projects may fail before their loan and mortgage periods are up) the investor is not required to repay the loan [...] In effect, the subsidies are not housing programs as much as they are investment programs with housing as a sideline."

"You can return your entire capital in a little more than two years," Yorke griped, in the *Sun,* "it's almost a license to print money."

By December of 1974, Vancouver's rental vacancy rate had slipped to an unheard-of 0.1%, and following the shouting match at Kitsilano High School, Yorke and the Tenants Union stepped up their game. The revised Landlord and Tenant Act became law in 1974, but it wasn't without its problems; while it did include rent control, many dwellings were exempt, including units renting for more than five hundred dollars per month, buildings containing two or more units, or ones also occupied by the landlord. The creation of a "Rentalsman's Office" had been similarly unhelpful, with Department Head Jim Patterson simply going along with the real estate industry's demands (which included a 30% rent hike in 1975).

Thanks to pressure from the BCTU, Patterson lasted just three months on the job.

"Finally, after we presented a petition with twenty-five thousand names to the provincial government, it acted and took the rent-setting authority out of the hands of the rentalsman and placed it in the hands of a Rent Review Commission," Yorke explained. "Rent increases for 1975 were also limited to 10.6%. The petition and the associated activities led by our tenant movement at this time were probably the high point of our entire activity."

But it wouldn't last.

In 1975, the Social Credit government of W.A.C. Bennett was re-elected, and began to slowly dismantle rent control. On August 17, 1977, they introduced the Residential Tenancy Act, which superseded the NDP's 1974 legislation, greatly increasing the number of buildings exempt from rent control; this included all new construction, and lowered the per-month eligibility amount from five hundred dollars to four hundred dollars.

"The Social Credit government kept its promises to landlords who helped elect it," Yorke said, bitterly, in 1978. "The only tenants that really have any protection are those who have remained on the same premises year after year, since they know the legal rent level and the frequency of increases permitted. Enforcement of this legislation remains very poor. The Rent Review Commission has been absorbed by the rentalsman's office. His office has, in fact, become a sort of auxiliary to the landlords, personnel and administrative."

Then, in 1984, the Bennett government removed rent controls altogether, once again allowing landlords to raise rents at their discretion, and evict tenants without cause. MLAs argued that it would stimulate development, bring investment, and increase the amount of available supply.

"It's fair to say that this government identified this particular time as a window in which we could move to let the marketplace work," said Consumer and Corporate Affairs Minister Jim Hewitt, "and allow renters the opportunity to have available to them rental accommodation and have competition as opposed to government intervention in the marketplace ... the competition of the marketplace will determine what price a person pays for an apartment. That's the way it should be. The marketplace should be allowed to work."

Public condemnation was swift, forcing the Social Credit government to backtrack on several legislative provisions, including eviction without cause, but otherwise, rent control had been effectively eliminated from BC's real estate landscape. In this, the government had been firmly directed by provincial business interests, in particular, a newly-formed "advocacy group" calling itself the Fraser Institute. Formed by corporate money (in particular, forestry giant MacMillan Bloedel) in response to the election of the Barrett NDP, the Institute had never met a free-market cause it wouldn't champion, and quickly elbowed its way into the public discourse on issues like corporate tax cuts, curbing the minimum wage, privatized healthcare, and even tobacco industry deregulation. Walter Block, the Institute's senior economist from 1979–1991, was also its regular mouthpiece in local newspapers, and throughout the 1980s, had come out as a staunch opponent of rent control.

"Rent Control is a policy that still bedevils modern society," Block wrote, in a 1989 article for the *Mid-Atlantic Journal of Business,* "British Columbia is the only jurisdiction in the entire world in the last 30 years which has eliminated its rent control. It has done so, moreover, without suffering any deleterious effects. Because of its un-happy previous experiences with rent control, this enactment has long been viewed unfavorably by the majority of the citizenry of British Columbia" (incidentally, among Block's other expert opinions were the fact that slavery was "not so bad — you pick cotton and sing songs," and that women and people of colour are paid less because they're generally "less productive").

"[W]hat we have in British Columbia in terms of the Residential Tenancy Act and regulations," sighed MLA Robin Blencoe, in the legislature, "[is] not coming from some of the saner members of the government. It's coming from that weird and wonderful group, the Fraser Institute. They are the ones who are directing the government these days."

And in their campaign against rent control, they had served their donors well — in particular, the real estate industry. Immediately after controls were lifted, the city's average rents went up by fifteen per cent. It would be more than ten years before the province reexamined rent control, and ultimately, a UBC study would conclude that the removal of controls had in no way led to an increase in housing supply.

INTERLUDE:
Real Estate and Race (Part II)

David Lam had taken a gamble.

It was a speculative investment in the future — specifically, his own. The year was 1967, and Lam (with his wife Dorothy and their two daughters) had opted to leave his cushy position as the manager of a successful Hong Kong bank, to start a new life in Canada. Lam's had been a privileged existence; coming from a wealthy family (the bank where he worked was owned by his parents), he had spent his youth surrounded by servants, driving luxury automobiles, and consorting with the city's business elite. Affable and hard-working, Lam had received a master's degree from Temple University, and seemed on track to continue in the family business, until, during one of his many travels abroad, he fell in love with a sleepy little city in the Pacific Northwest: Vancouver.

With all of his assets tied up back home, Lam's first few years in the city were lean ones — though not so lean the family couldn't purchase a corner lot on Ash Street. By the time he arrived, Lam had turned his attention away from the banking sector, and toward the world of real estate — a world that, to his eye, held untold potential. As a student with a Western education, Lam knew that, for much of the past century, Chinese-Canadians had been subject to all manner of discrimination, and that, in North America, real estate had been used as a tool to advance that racist agenda. However, by the 1960s, attitudes in Vancouver were slowly changing — particularly within the business community, where international deals with Asia were opening up new possibilities for profit. To Lam's surprise, although he and his family were the neighbourhood's first Chinese-Canadian residents, their neighbours welcomed them with open arms.

"Our neighbours," he later told his biographer, "were just out of this world."

And those attitudes extended into the workplace; in addition to his tireless work ethic, one of Lam's many skills was an aptitude for making friends, and in short order, he had talked his way into a job as a real estate salesman at a firm down the street from his home. While his days were spent on the job, hustling for commissions, his nights were devoted to learning as much about the real estate profession as he could. As a student in UBC's Faculty of Commerce, he quickly advanced his education until he had not only earned a degree, but a place as a fellow at the Real Estate Institute of British Columbia. Lam passed his licensing exam in 1969, and earned his first commission selling a home to his friend Fung King-Hey — for which he made a paltry four hundred dollars. Although excited by the money — the first he had made in Canada — Lam wasn't content with a mere salesman's earnings.

Then, he had a brainwave.

"I suddenly came across one word," he later recalled, "matchmaker. You have money and I have opportunity for you."

And the people with the money, Lam realized, were overseas investors — many of whom were his old associates in the Hong

Kong business community. Rather than selling houses one at a time, Lam knew that the profit potential was much greater if he acted instead as a bridge between Vancouver and Asia, a broker who could link money with opportunity — in particular, the opportunities provided by Vancouver's relatively cheap, largely unregulated real estate market.

Lam's first such deal was a property on North Road, between the municipalities of Burnaby and Coquitlam. Together, he and Fung (to whom he'd sold his first house) brought together more than a dozen Hong Kong associates to purchase and develop the lot (which later won an award for architecture). He named the development Sunnyside Estates (the name of Lam's projects invariably contained the word "Sunny," to dispel investor notions of Vancouver's wet climate), and it would be the first of many.

By the end of the 1960s, Lam had developed a solid roster of Hong Kong clients, and continued to bring in more — from Hong Kong, Singapore, Kuala Lumpur, and the Arab Emirates. By this time, he had left his sales job to work for Wall & Redekop, who saw Lam's potential for attracting global capital, and named him the president of their international division. Lam was also making a considerable amount off his own real estate deals, at one point having enough capital to loan Wall & Redekop half a million dollars. And in addition to his overseas contacts, Lam made friends with a series of Canadian heavy-hitters, among them Jack Poole. In 1972, the duo became partners on a development project in Calgary, making a deal that closed in a single afternoon.

But then, in 1972, the NDP government of premier Dave Barrett took power.

Barrett, a former social worker and civil servant, had been the first provincial premier to make rent control part of his election platform, and once elected, began working toward updating the

Landlord and Tenant Act as one of a series of worker-focused, regulatory reforms. These reforms spooked the overseas business community — among them, Lam's clients, and for a time, Lam turned his attention toward the American market (although this didn't stop him from arranging the sale of half of an apartment building near Stanley Park to a consortium of investors from Hong Kong, Singapore, and Kuala Lumpur). As the city of Vancouver began to demand more concessions from developers in the rental apartment game, Lam also began to purchase and redevelop shopping centres, doing renovations and removing less successful vendors before reselling the properties at a profit. Then, in 1974, as Vancouver's property market boomed, Lam took part in his largest deal to date: the purchase of the Board of Trade and Baxter buildings in downtown Vancouver. His client was Geoffrey Lau, heir to a Hong Kong-based commercial empire who was looking to keep his family's money out of the hands of the Chinese government. Thanks to Lam's diligence, he succeeded. The sale was one of the largest in Canada at the time (outside of Toronto), as well as one of the biggest deals ever to involve money from the Far East.

At this point, Lam struck out on his own. And he never looked back. Through his own company, Canadian International Properties, he continued to build his real estate empire, acting as a broker, property manager, and developer, and by the late 1970s, his clients included many of the richest men in Hong Kong. And although his business ventures did generally reap windfall profits, Lam, a devout Christian, was publicly circumspect about the profit motive itself.

"I was told by a well-known economist that the only business of business is to make a profit," he told an audience at the United Way in 1988. "I pondered on this saying and was shocked by it.

What a horrible world ours will become if the only business of our business is to make money. I would say the business of business is to serve, to make a better world for everyone, and in the process, hopefully, you will make some money."

David Lam at the Chinese Cultural Centre, 1987
(CVA AM1523-S6-F44). Photo by Paul Yee. COV copyright.

And this was more than simple lip service; when units sold poorly in one of Lam's apartment buildings across from the Vancouver General Hospital on 12th Avenue, Lam made up the investors' shortfall with his own money.

By the early 1980s, he was looking toward retirement. And after extricating himself from the more than a dozen companies in which he owned a stake, Lam turned to philanthropy. In this, he continued to act as a bridge between Canada and Asia; although he had, in his own estimation, personally experienced very little racism in Canada, he spoke out about it in many public addresses — not just educating Canadian citizens, but new Chinese arrivals. He and his wife Dorothy formed their own charitable foundation in 1985, and he made donations to all manner of causes and local institutions (including the University of British Columbia and the Vancouver Police Museum, among many others).

Then, in 1986, Lam received one of the province's highest honours, when he was named the twenty-fifth Lieutenant Governor of British Columbia. For many in BC's political class, the appointment was a surprise. But for Lam, it was the culmination of decades of hard work, something that symbolized the crucial role that Asia-Pacific trade would play in the province of the future, and that Lam had been an integral part of bringing it about. Almost twenty years after he had arrived, Lam's gamble had paid off. But, a few years earlier — immediately following his retirement — Lam had accepted another offer. It was to take part in a delegation that involved all three levels of government, something for which his years of experience were uniquely and perfectly suited. His success as a matchmaker hadn't gone unnoticed. And now, the province of BC wanted to make a few matches of their own.

It would come to be known as the "Pacific Strategy", and like the Strata Titles Act of almost twenty years before, it was set to change Vancouver's landscape forever.

RED
(1984 – Present)

"It is worrisome to learn that newly-built housing developments in Vancouver are being sold on the international market without being offered for sale in Vancouver. Vancouver suffers from a housing shortage, especially of affordable housing. If prices are driven up to international levels and marketed solely abroad, Vancouver buyers will be excluded... Statements to the effect that Vancouver must also follow this international trend or face the wrath of international investors and developers are one-sided. Whose concerns ought to take precedence? What is Vancouver if it is not a city for Vancouverites?"

— **Letter to the Editor,** *Vancouver Sun*, **1989**

17.

THE REGATTA

"Vancouver's beauty, livability, and strategic location makes it one of the most sought after areas in the world to live. As such, the demand of foreign buyers for this precious real estate will cause not only diminished availability but also a crisis in affordable housing for the average British Columbian."

— Gordon Wilson, December 1988

ON DECEMBER 14 of 1988, the *Vancouver Sun* ran the following item on its front page:

"Backlash feared as condos sold to Hong Kong residents," the headline read.

Then below: "Hong Kong residents buying property in Vancouver face a backlash from Canadians because a growing number of developments are being marketed here without being offered in Canada. At least half a dozen Lower Mainland developments have been sold here recently without being offered to Vancouver residents."

The development in question was known as The Regatta.

Near the edge of the False Creek basin, the condo tower sat on a tiny corner of the Expo Lands — a massive swathe of property recently purchased from the BC government by a newly-minted development company calling itself Concord Pacific — in which virtually every one of its 216 units were sold to overseas speculators in a period of just three hours.

As the paper predicted, backlash was swift.

Before the day was out, public pressure forced Municipal Affairs Minister Rita Johnson to sit down with Concord Pacific's vice president, Victor Li, and demand answers. At first, Li was defensive and non-committal, complaining that "20 other condominium developments in Vancouver were being sold in Hong Kong at the same time as his and yet his sale has been the only one to get publicity." Company spokesman Craig Aspinall was similarly combative, blaming unease about foreign ownership and a hostile local climate for the trouble, and giving vague assurances that BC buyers would get first crack at the next set of Concord Pacific developments (stopping well short of a personal guarantee from Li). Concord Pacific had already followed the same pattern with their two hundred-unit Cambridge Garden project, which was also sold entirely to Hong Kong buyers, and swapped through a network of other Li-owned companies. When pressed, Aspinall offered the excuse that the overseas sales were due to clerical error.

"Someone forgot to account for the time-zone changes," he said.

But in the days that followed, as the outcry grew louder, the city, the province, and Concord's executives went into damage-control mode.

Pressure got to be so intense that Li had a meeting with acting Vancouver Mayor Carole Taylor, who demanded an assurance that properties would be sold to local buyers first, at a fair local price. Li took to the papers, apologizing for marketing The Regatta in Hong Kong only, assuring skittish Vancouverites that local prices would indeed be offered to local buyers, and maintaining that speculators would only be able to purchase one unit each.

"I admit, although I have not broken any laws or normal business codes or ethics," he told the *Sun*, huffily, in early January, "I was not being sensitive to local feelings."

"The negative implications of not following through would be too great for them," added Victor Yang, president of the Hong Kong-Canada Business Association. "Either they keep their mouths shut or they're obligated to follow through." The Li family, he added, had "learned to be sensitive" to the needs of the local market.

This would prove to be untrue.

Within two weeks, word was already circulating that Concord Pacific would be parcelling out its holdings to other developers, none of which would be bound by Li's guarantees. Before construction was complete, four Regatta units were put back on the market at twice their price. And ultimately, local buyers would be given just a twenty-four-hour window to make their purchases, after which all efforts would turn toward the Hong Kong market.

"Pretty soon, you will have a property market in Vancouver that runs irrespective of local buyers," warned property analyst Rick Gossen, in the *Sun*. "There will be developments that don't have to cater to local people, because they can sell out in Hong Kong. Unfortunately, it could bring on a backlash from Canadians, who can become less important in setting prices of some developments in their own city."

"Vancouver was caught off-guard by the magnitude of interest by Asians in the town's residential real estate," noted an article in the *Chinatown News*, "enough interest — some would call it a feeding frenzy — to create a property boom divorced from the generally unimpressive BC economy... A recent survey by the *Sun* placed the amount of Asian buying of total property sales at 30 percent in October [1988]; 25% of total property sales by Hong Kong residents."

These comments were quickly countered by allegations of racism in the pages of local papers and by Concord itself, as well as real estate organizations and free enterprise think tanks like the Fraser Institute.

"The Regatta issue is not one of race, but focuses on a perceived slight of Canadians who have little input to property development in their own backyard," Gossen later wrote, in the *South China Morning Post*. "From a commercial standpoint, the units were marketed where they could be sold most efficiently (in Hong Kong) with the most high profile company (Cheung Kong). In Vancouver, government officials offer non-commercial reasons saying that the units should be offered locally."

Although Vancouverites didn't yet realize it, the situation went far deeper than just The Regatta.

The emergence of Concord Pacific, and their development of the Expo Lands marked a turning point in the history of the city, one that would dictate much of its subsequent growth — even into the present day — a story involving unsavoury characters, idealogical battles, backroom dealings, and a controversial sale to the richest man in China. Vancouver's speculators, developers, and rentier capitalists had jumped into bed with a whole new syndicate, one capable of playing for much higher stakes. But more than anything else, the Regatta incident marked the beginning of a public discussion that has continued — in more or less this exact form — for more than thirty years, a debate about global capital and foreign investment, about affordability and race, regulation and the free market.

But then, as now, several key points were missing from that mainstream debate: first — like Li — many of the investors weren't technically foreign.

Second, they were invited.

18.

THE PACIFIC STRATEGY

*"That our real estate is much lower priced than
that in the countries from which the investors
come (Germany, Iran, China, etc) coupled with
the benefit on exchange, encouraged foreign
buyers to pay any price asked, thus raising
prices for all real estate... The foreign buyers
pay cash and buy quickly. The result is that
residents of BC can no longer afford residential
real estate. That is a shocking situation."*

— Letter to the Editor, *Vancouver Sun*, November 25, 1980

BY THE EARLY 1980s, British Columbia's economy was in serious
trouble.

Despite significant growth between 1976 and 1980, a global market
downturn had plunged BC into the worst recession it had experienced
since the Great Depression.

Then, in late 1981, the housing market crashed. Home prices

dropped by an unheard-of forty per cent. Inside of a year, unemployment doubled. The provincial economy shrunk by eight per cent in
1982 alone, and the resource sectors that had formerly been a corner-
stone of economic growth fell apart. Just prior to the crash,
speculative investment in Vancouver housing had hit an all-time
high, with roughly twenty per cent of all home purchases in a six-
month period made for the purpose of speculation. The situation
had led Consumer and Corporate Affairs Minister Peter Hyndman
to introduce the Real Estate Amendment Act in Victoria, aimed at
curbing speculative buying by requiring increased transparency from
both buyers and salespeople.

The crash rendered this unnecessary.

In the months that followed, the crumbling market hit Vancouver's
major developers hard, but for Jack Poole's Daon Developments, it
proved to be especially catastrophic. Part of the company's aggressive
expansion strategy relied on being perpetually overleveraged, and by
1986, plummeting sales and a twenty per cent interest rate had left
Daon more than two billion in debt (to forty-seven different banks).
Somehow, Poole managed to negotiate a deal with his creditors (paying them a portion in shares instead of cash), but in the process, was
forced to lay off most of his staff, vacate his "Golden Tower" headquarters, and sell all of his assets, including his private jet, his Idaho
retreat, and his home in West Vancouver.

By 1983, with unemployment at fourteen per cent, and having
just narrowly avoided a province-wide general strike, Prime Minister
Pierre Trudeau, and BC's Social Credit government began working
desperately to reboot the economy in the only way they knew how:
by marketing BC as an investment destination. Dubbed the Pacific
Strategy, it involved all three levels of government courting investment from one of the largest, and fastest-growing economies in the
world: Asia — and in particular, China. In addition to encouraging
corporate involvement, Ottawa began ostensibly selling Canadian

citizenship through a scheme known as the Business Investor Program. Started in the 1970s and expanded in 1986 (in part to help BC, the province hardest-hit by the recession), the BIP allowed immigrant investors to receive an expedited passport if they had a net worth of more than $800,000, and agreed to loan half of that to the provincial government for a period of five years, interest-free. Entrepreneurs had an even easier time, being required to invest a mere $150,000, and hire just one Canadian employee for their business.

Although the wooing of Pacific Rim trade had begun more than ten years earlier, Canadian officials had stepped up their game by the 1980s, sending regular delegations from the federal, provincial, and civic levels (to the point that provincial premiers even went so far as to divide China into territories for their trade missions). It was a far cry from the social and economic exclusionism of the early-to-mid twentieth century; in March of 1985, a civic delegation that included then-Mayor Mike Harcourt travelled to Hong Kong, and their objectives, according to a City of Vancouver report, were:

> To establish Vancouver's commitment to fostering two-way trade and investment, as well as a full range of linkages and relationships with the Asian Pacific Rim.

> To promote a broader awareness of business and investment opportunities in Vancouver and its regional hinterland; and to explore the possibilities of private investment and joint ventures in the Asian Pacific Rim.

> To assist in the marketing of Vancouver's specialized services and 'invisible exports' — financial services, business, trade, and professional services and tourism.

"In this, Mayor Harcourt joins the growing multitude of North American hi-zoners obsequiously smiling their way through the economic dynamos of Asia," griped the *Sun*'s Pete McMartin. "Brochures in one hand, hat in the other, they go there on pilgrimage hoping for the economic kiss of life... But I often get the feeling that we are looking at the Pacific Rim as something other than a new market. Has a group of capitalists ever been wooed more desperately for their spare change? We see Japan and Hong Kong and Singapore, to all appearance generating vibrant, robust economies out of ether and sweat, and we look on with nostalgic envy."

But from a trade perspective, it worked; before the end of the 1980s, trade with Asia had outpaced trade with Europe for the first time in history. However there was still one crucial piece of the Pacific Strategy that had yet to be implemented, one that would, in the eyes of its proponents, cement Vancouver's legacy on the world stage, a piece of place marketing that would have exceeded Walter Gravely's wildest dreams: a world's fair.

When the gates first opened in May of 1986, few could debate that Expo was the most extravagant celebration Vancouver had ever seen. Taking place over 165 days, involving fifty-four countries, twenty-two million attendees, 173 acres of fairground, and bringing in $491 million in revenue, the fair was viewed as an unqualified success, responsible for a fifteen per cent bump in the government's approval rating, and subsequently handing the Social Credit party one of the largest electoral victories in provincial history. At first, the fair (originally known as "Transpo 86") was slated to be a relatively modest endeavour — eighty million dollars in expenditures, to celebrate Vancouver's centennial and secure federal funds for infrastructure(including a convention centre, a stadium, and a rapid transit line). But before long, it had been co-opted to market Vancouver as a destination for real estate investment — one which was both inexpensive and virtually unregulated.

The effects of this decision were felt almost instantly, and nowhere more acutely than in the city's most vulnerable neighbourhood: the Downtown East Side.

As early as 1983, neighbourhood advocates like Lookout's Karen O'Shannacery and Jim Green (of the Downtown East Side Resident's Association) began speaking out against what they suspected would be a slew of Expo-related evictions, as SRO hotel owners removed their low-income tenants to cash in on lucrative tourist traffic. Before 1988, SROs weren't included under Residential Tenancy Branch legislation, meaning that landlords had virtual carte blanche to evict tenants, raise rents, or charge additional fees at their discretion. All disputes went to small claims court, a process which took far too long for most low-income residents, and handed even more power to property owners. Fearing the worst, Green, O'Shannacery, and other members of DERA researched world's fair events all over the world. They lobbied all three levels of government, as well as Expo officials, pleading for rent freezes and no-evictions clauses. They made presentations to city hall, and chaired public meetings. They even came up with specific policy ideas, in collaboration with the city's Social Planning Department. At every level they were ignored.

"Our members have no intention of evicting tenants or making unjustified rate increases in time for Expo," claimed the BC Hotel Association's Rick Higgs, in a 1985 interview with the *Eastender*.

NPA Alderman Gordon Campbell scoffed at the idea, accusing advocates of "trying to set up a bunch of straw men and burn them down."

This was, at best, ignorant.

Between 1984 and 1986, more than seven hundred people were evicted from the Downtown East Side — all of them on some form of social assistance. And as Expo drew nearer, the official response to the displacements grew even more callous. Quoted in the *New York Times*, Premier Bennett praised the idea, calling it "a once in a generation chance to redevelop what has become a seedy slum." Social Credit advisor Michael Walker suggested that Downtown East Side residents could "save everyone a lot of trouble if they all were put on buses to the Kootenays. The world runs by greed. Everyone is greedy in one way or another. What we're talking about is relative greed. It's not a question of dire necessity. It's a question of choice of location. People are saying 'I don't want to live in the Kootenays ... I want to live where the action is.'"

"It may seem insignificant to most people, but the impact Expo had on the Downtown East Side was devastating," O'Shannacery later explained. "It was incredibly personally devastating. We had people in tears when they got those notices [...] "These weren't hotel rooms that people were renting for the night. These were people's homes. They'd be living an average of 20–30 years there. It was the second most stable community in Vancouver after the Dunbar area. This was a home. People knew each other. There was always a huge sense of community."

Despite aggressive lobbying, no rent-control provisions were ever enacted. No anti-eviction clauses were mandated. Left with few options, many SRO residents were forced into lower-quality hotels. Others had to return to shelters, or were faced with abandoning their community and being shipped to the suburbs. Some committed suicide. By the end of 1986, at least eleven deaths were directly related to the displacements, including fifty-year-old Daniel Stephen Ponak, who leapt from his window after being evicted from the Patricia Hotel, and eighty-eight-year-old Olaf Solheim, who starved to death weeks after having his door torn off for refusing to leave his room.

"Expo 86 killed people," O'Shannacery later said. "It killed people in the Downtown East Side. They wanted to duck that, but it's real. And knowing some of those people, it's real to me. Thirty years later, it's real to me. That should not happen."

"If you take an older person who's been living in the same room for 30–40 years, you don't realize that the impact of a displacement — or even a careful relocation — can be absolutely devastating," added retired housing advocate Judy Graves, who worked in the neighbourhood during the fair. "As long as they're in the same room, they know where to find the Harbour Light food line, they know where to find their doctor. But you move them down the block, where they have to turn a different direction, they're completely lost. You can go back a month later and find they haven't eaten."

DERA research later revealed that ultimately, none of the city's SRO hotels made any money from Expo tourist traffic. But the fate of residents like Solheim did finally spur changes at the provincial level; in December of 1988, after more than fifteen years of campaigning by advocates like Green and O'Shannacery, the province decided to include SROs in Residential Tenancy Branch legislation. Despite the crowing of politicians and the business elite, Expo wasn't a financial success, closing with a $311 million deficit — one paid off through the creation of Lotto 6/49.

And although Expo rolled out a plush welcome mat for wealthy investors, it was the Business Investor Program that truly got them through the door. Combined, the Pacific Strategy, Expo, and the BIP created a perfect storm in Vancouver real estate, serving as the catlyst for a generation of housing injustice; between 1980 and 2001, at least 330,000 people utilized the scheme, and with Vancouver was the most popular landing destination (far ahead of Toronto). Of those who invested in BC, two-thirds were from Taiwan, South Korea, and Hong Kong — in large part because of a desire to export capital before the return of Hong Kong to Communist rule. While, on paper, the BIP was created to serve entrepreneurs and skilled workers as well as investors, the program disproportionately favoured the wealthy, and it wasn't long before they had found ways to abuse it. Since it was geared more toward attracting capital than business, investors had the easiest time purchasing citizenship; applicants were graded on a 100-point scale, taking into account factors such as income and education, but while those in the "skilled worker" category needed to score a minimum of sixty-seven points, investors needed just thirty-five. As a result, and because BC's property market was far more attractive for new arrivals than its business environment, rife with onerous regulations, the BIP accomplished very little, other than creating a class of wealthy, non-resident property owners; while roughly forty per cent of BIP participants were property owners within six months of arrival, only sixty-two per cent had any intention of working within the country. In fact, a 1989 audit by Price Waterhouse found that many of those involved in the program didn't even comply with its most basic conditions; of those surveyed by the company, fifty per cent didn't respond at all, and of those who did, half weren't meeting BIP terms. To make matters worse, while the program unquestionably benefited the wealthy, it did very little for actual working immigrants. By 1992, according to the Price Waterhouse audit, roughly half of BIP participants still couldn't be located, and of those who could, only one-third were actually working within the country. Business owners didn't fare much better, with just thirty-five per cent of the enterprises started under the program turning a profit. A subsequent Ernst and Young audit concluded that the BIP's "success is much more limited than is suggested by gross estimates of numbers of immigrant investors, or their gross investment," and by 1999, a senior auditor with the World Bank labelled it "[a] massive sham."

But at the same time, the effect on the city's real estate market was profound; between 1986 and 1991, Metro Vancouver's population grew by sixteen per cent.

During roughly the same period (1986–1995), property values more than doubled.

The program was finally halted at the federal level in 2014, at which time the backlog for applicants sat at almost sixty thousand — all of them with a net worth of at least three-quarters of a million dollars. But there was one more reason for the massive influx of global capital in the wake of Expo.

Because the Pacific Strategy had not only put Vancouver on the map, but had also attracted the attention of one of the richest men in the entire world, an enigmatic merchant who had spent decades building an empire from nothing, a de facto national hero known affectionately as "Mr. Money."

His name was Li Ka-Shing. And he had big plans.

19.

THE SALE

"There is a fearful housing crisis in Vancouver. That speculative investment, much of it by offshore investors, is part of the problem is demonstrably apparent."

— Denny Boyd, February 23, 1989

IN THE SPRING of 1988, the Province of British Columbia handed 15.2 million square feet on the False Creek basin — one-sixth of the downtown peninsula, and the largest remaining undeveloped parcel of land in Vancouver — over to a twenty-three-year-old Stanford student with no previous development experience. With just fifty million dollars down, the senior vice president of Concord Pacific was now responsible for one of the largest private development projects in North America, a neighbourhood set to be built from the ground up, comprising forty towers, eighty-five hundred suites, and 3.5 million square feet of commercial space.

"...[E]verything from the height of skyscrapers to housing for the poor suddenly revolves around the mysterious figure of the Hong Kong billionaire," the *Sun* noted, in December of 1988.

He hadn't even graduated.

His name was Victor Li, and he was the son of the richest man in China.

Slight, with dark hair and thick glasses, Li was said to have little regard for the Canadian press, or his identity in Canada, preferring instead to keep a low profile and let his work — what little of it there was at the time — speak for itself. Despite his inexperience, Li was placed at the helm of Concord Pacific, nestled amongst a group of highly-trained managers to guide him.

His father, Li Ka-Shing, was a true rags-to-riches story. Having escaped communist China at a young age, he had managed to parlay a small business making plastic flowers into an international empire, with diversified assets that included hotels, telecommunications, oil and gas, dockyards, and massive amounts of commercial and residential real estate. He was a mysterious figure; like his son, he jealously guarded his privacy, giving few interviews, and appearing in even fewer photos. By the early 1980s, his personal wealth had passed the two-billion-dollar mark, and with two of his sons — Richard and Victor — nearing the end of their respective Ivy League educations, he was looking to expand his empire.

At which point, the BC government stepped in and made him an offer he couldn't refuse.

After the end of Expo, and with another recession looming, the province had begun to look for ways to sell off their land holdings as quickly as possible. To that end, they had formed the British Columbia Enterprise Corporation, a public/private entity created to dispose of the land and other assets on the government's behalf.

And while an official shortlist of bidders was assembled in the fall of 1987, the process had begun long before that. It was no secret that the development of the Expo lands would be extraordinarily lucrative, and as such, different factions began to form within the halls of government, the BCEC, and the world of private enterprise — each with their own agenda.

Like the CPR grant a century earlier, the bidding process was neither aboveboard nor particularly transparent. For a start, the land was put on the market as a single entity, a decision which crowded out all but the biggest players in the market — excluding even local big fish like Jack Poole and Jimmy Pattison. On top of that, two former BCEC board members — Peter Toigo and Stanley Kwok — were directly involved in the bidding process, having resigned their seats shortly before it was set to begin. Kwok had also been the president of BC Place Corporation since 1984, working in development in False Creek during the pre-Expo years. Following his resignation, Toigo immediately began putting together a bid of his own, using inside information from his time at BCEC, and his close friendship with then-Premier Bill Vander Zalm. Kwok, meanwhile, took a cushy job as a vice president at Concord Pacific, alongside Victor Li.

In September of 1987, BCEC President Kevin Murphy paid Li a visit, and in the months that followed, two camps coalesced — one advocating for Li (which included Murphy, Provincial Secretary Grace McCarthy, and BCEC Chairman Peter Brown), and the other pushing for Toigo (including Vander Zalm and his aide/personal friend David Poole).

It got vicious.

Uneasy with Toigo's close relationship with the premier, and the inside information it had provided regarding the land's value, McCarthy took the matter to the provincial attorney general, who immediately opened an investigation (of less concern to all involved was the fact that the government's own independent valuation was done by Burns Fry, a company recently employed by Li Ka-Shing). At the same time, Murphy, Brown, and McCarthy were meeting regularly with both Li Sr., and his son Victor; Brown had even entertained Victor and other Concord Pacific employees at his Point Grey home in September of 1987. It's unclear what was discussed, but it's likely that Brown and Li Jr. would have had plenty to talk about. Both came from unbelievably privileged backgrounds — Li as the heir to a business empire, and Brown from a dynasty that had begun with his grandfather Brenton — the same Brenton Brown who had co-founded the NPA. Like Vander Zalm, Toigo, and many of the others involved, Brown was a man for whom "unscrupulous" would be a charitable description.

"Look back to your school days," a family friend explained, in 1989. "Remember the schoolyard bully. Very insecure. Spends his time beating up and belittling others. Brown's just like that. Most of his actions are rooted in contempt for the other guy."

Brown's tactics would have made the Wolf of Wall Street proud; newspaper profiles of the day noted his seventy pairs of Gucci loafers, or his habit of measuring his trading days in bottles of Dom Perignon. He also owned more than four thousand apartment units, and a one-fifth stake in the resort city of Whistler. Brown specialized in making money, but his methods usually involved screwing over both clients and other investors; his specialty was pump-and-dump schemes, whereby promoters artificially inflated the value of stocks — many of which he personally underwrote — and then walked away when they crashed. During Brown's tenure as head of the Vancouver Stock Exchange, it came to be labelled the "scam capital of the world" and a "Cesspool" by the May, 29, 1989 edition of *Forbes*. "The VSE, founded in 1907, is the longest-standing joke in North America," the magazine noted, "the Cubs included."

Nonetheless, the meetings continued, and by the middle of 1988, the attorney general's investigation had forced Toigo to withdraw from the process, leaving Li as the sole remaining bidder.

"We were concerned," he told the *Sun*, "but not worried because we felt our project was a winning project and our price was a fair price."

In fact, the government gave him a sweetheart of a deal.

The sale, announced on April 29, 1987, gave Concord Pacific the Expo Lands for a mere $145 million — fifty million dollars down, with the remainder to be paid out between 1995 and 2003. Critics of the sale, including Toigo, and the NDP's Steven Cox, were aghast, noting that this was a valuation of just ten dollars per square foot (at the time, West End condos were selling for between sixty to eighty dollars per square foot).

The cost of cleaning up False Creek's industrial waste, meanwhile, was left to taxpayers, to the tune of seventy-five million dollars. The contract also contained a no-flipping clause — although this only applied to the land as a whole, and had no restrictions around parcelling it off to other developers. Later assessments of the Expo lands would place its value at approximately one billion dollars, leading Peter Toigo to go on record in July of 1988, complaining that Li Ka-Shing "stole" the property.

"I had nothing against Li Ka-Shing and congratulate him on his success," he griped. "If he was capable of stealing the property, good luck to him."

Jack Poole wasn't happy either; in the spring of 1988, he contacted a lawyer to explore his options, and expressed "grave misgivings" about the process in the pages of the *Vancouver Sun*.

The political fallout surrounding the deal was considerable. BC Liberal Party leader Gordon Wilson demanded a judicial inquiry into the terms of the sale, and former Mayor Mike Harcourt — as leader of the official opposition — requested the entire site be bought back from the company. In the face of public pressure, Vander Zalm flailed spectacularly; first, he made the ridiculous assertion that he hadn't read the entire contract. Then, he talked of renegotiating the deal altogether (impossible by that point, since it had already been finalized), but after a meeting with Victor Li, changed his tune again, claiming he had never intended to reopen the discussion. The bungle cost Vander Zalm's government dearly; in the provincial election that followed, the party virtually disappeared, and Vander Zalm himself later resigned after another conflict-of-interest scandal involving land, global investors, influence peddling, and literal bags of cash.

As for Victor Li, he kept the same low profile he always had, although he did manage to get cozy with a number of government figures, including Prime Minister Kim Campbell, Premiers Mike Harcourt and Gordon Campbell, and civic politicians like Libby Davies and Grace McCarthy.

In 1990, Concord Pacific sold 4.2 hectares of the Expo lands to an unnamed Singapore tycoon for forty million dollars, essentially recouping their initial investment. Later in 1990, the company sold a further thirty-five per cent to a Taiwanese company, for two hundred million dollars. Despite Li's prior assurances, Pacific Place, a Concord Pacific development, was marketed primarily in Hong Kong. By 1993, Li returned to Hong Kong himself, leaving much of Concord Pacific's work to longtime friend Terry Hui. In 1996, he resigned altogether, to focus exclusively on overseas development.

More than any other single event, the sale of the Expo lands forever changed the trajectory of Vancouver real estate. Where Li Ka-Shing went, other investors followed, and between 1988 and 1997, the city gained an estimated fifty billion dollars in wealth, directly from the international business elite. During a single week in 1992, according to David Ley's estimates, fifty millionaires opened bank accounts at the Chinatown branch of HSBC, and in 1995 alone, five hundred million dollars was wired from Hong Kong to BC. A 1988 industry estimate by the Hong Kong Canada Business Association estimated that at least thirty Vancouver building projects weren't sold in Canada at all. Hand-in-hand with single detached homes were presale condos, a concept introduced by Concord Pacific's VPs, and aggressively refined by local marketers and realtors — in particular, Bob Rennie — to target overseas buyers.

"In B.C. we have a paradox," wrote the *Sun*'s Eric Downton, "one that our politicians and business leaders would rather not talk about. The provincial government and the private sector are spending large sums of money to lure Asian investment and well-heeled immigrants to B.C. Throughout Eastern Asia our representatives are flaunting the welcome mat. 'Come to beautiful British Columbia! The sky's the limit for economic opportunity!' The main targets of such blandishments are Japan, South Korea, Taiwan, and the Chinese business communities in Hong Kong, Singapore, and Malaysia. The campaign is going well. Ironically, its success is feeding the anti-Asian backlash, the closet racism."

Indeed, by 1989, with the influx of money from Hong Kong, the discourse around real estate and racism had intensified. On a weekly, and sometimes daily basis, it was being debated in the press, by politicians, by independent experts and advocacy groups. But that debate, which had come to dominate the newspapers throughout the 1980s, had begun in a rather curious place. In fact, it could be traced to one specific study, conducted by one specific organization, and funded by one specific industry — one which first pushed the narrative, and had, in recent years, begun to steadily turn up the volume.

That industry was the real estate sector itself.

And their concerns were seemingly less about race than they were about profit.

INTERLUDE:
Real Estate and Race (Part III)

The Laurier Institution had made a gamble.

It was a speculative investment in the future — specifically, that of their donors. The year was 1989, and, if all went well, they were poised to change the narrative about real estate and race in Vancouver for decades. In the years following Li Ka-Shing's purchase of the Expo lands, debate around the role of Hong Kong money in Vancouver's market had continued to intensify; during a fifteen-month period between 1988 and early 1989, the *Sun* featured 189 stories containing the words "Hong Kong" and "Real Estate." Outside of real estate, racism was measurably present in the Vancouver of the late 1980s and early 1990s, with a Pew Global Attitudes survey finding that approximately five per cent of locals agreed with the statement: "Non-whites shouldn't be allowed to immigrate to Canada." During a 1989 meeting of the British/European Immigration Aid Foundation (one attended by former Mayor Jack Volrich), an attendee had labelled Chinese immigrants the "scum of the Earth," and was met with wild applause. Allegations of real estate racism appeared sporadically in the pages of local papers, coming from, among others, the pen of *Sun* columnist Jamie Lamb, and in editorials by Michael Goldberg, an academic specializing in urban land markets. In September 1988, in response to what reporters felt was discriminatory direction from their editorial department, the *Sun* held an in-house seminar on responsible reporting around race and immigration.

The Laurier Institution aimed to take that conversation one step further.

Founded in 1988 by a group that included millionaire financier Milton K. Wong, the institution billed itself as a "non-profit, non-advocacy research and education organization seeking to promote multiculturalism and ward off nativist tendencies," and made a point of its refusal to seek government funding, in order, it said, to retain its independence. Then, in 1990, a little over a year after its incorporation, the institution released a six-part series examining the role of Chinese immigration and capital on Vancouver's housing market.

It hit like a bombshell.

The study's lead author was a man named David Baxter, and the work was undertaken by the Canadian Real Estate Research Bureau, a group working out of the newly-formed Management Research Institute at UBC's Sauder School of Business. It was overseen by Michael Goldberg, the urban land markets expert often quoted in local newspapers newspapers, and dean of the Sauder School.

Spikes in the market, the study's authors wrote, were the result of interprovincial migration, and the spending habits of baby boomers — not Chinese immigration or global capital. Permit fees too were to blame, and fluctuations were well within the normal range.

"When that hit the press, it really and truly mitigated social conflict," Laurier founder Milton Wong later said, "[it] improved attitudes and ameliorated a lot of pressure even to this day."

There was just one problem: for all its talk of independence, the Laurier Institution — and its study — were underwritten by the real estate industry.

The Management Research Institute, where the study was prepared, had been funded in large part by David Lam — to the tune of ten million dollars. Lam had also donated an additional one million dollars toward a new library for the Faculty of Commerce, during a lunchtime meeting with Sauder Dean Michael Goldberg. Goldberg, who had overseen the project (and regularly opined about racism in real estate in the papers) also had extensive ties to real estate and development; in addition to being a personal friend of Lam's going back to the early 1980s, he had served on the board of directors at Wall & Redekop and, at the time the studies were released, was serving as governor and vice chairman of the BC Real Estate Foundation.

Perhaps most tellingly, while the Laurier report created a firestorm in the media, it received a very different response from real estate insiders.

"Within the real estate industry itself, the Laurier reports lacked credibility," explained UBC housing expert David Ley, in his book *Millionaire Migrants*, an exploration of global capital in Vancouver. "Laughter greeted the presentation of one report to an audience of realtors, while a prominent realtor dismissed the second report as 'naive.'"

In spite of this, the narrative stuck, remaining largely unchanged in the more than thirty years since the report's release. However, when it came to questions of racism, Vancouver's attitudes had changed considerably since the days of the Asiatic Exclusion League. Ley, who spent decades studying the housing phenomenon, put forth no small amount of effort to determine the true prevalence of racist attitudes amongst Vancouverites, and whether those attitudes were affecting discussions about the housing market. What he found was that Canadians generally have better attitudes about race relations than virtually any other country in the world — and of them, Vancouverites recorded the lowest percentage of racist opinions in the nation. According to the Pew Global Attitudes Project, seventy-seven per cent of Canadians agree with the statement: "Immigration yields more positive than negative outcomes"(no other country surveyed recorded agreement of more than fifty per cent). And in Vancouver, eighty per cent of locals agreed with the statement: "Immigration strengthens Canadian culture." While racism remains a factor in the day-to-day lives of Vancouverites, the expert consensus is that it's a much smaller part of the real estate conversation than the industry and its advocates would suggest, and that over the past thirty years rather than real estate being used to advance a racist agenda, racism is instead being used as a tool to advance a real estate agenda.

"It's a kind of moral signalling to camouflage immoral actions," scoffed Andy Yan, director of the City Program at Simon Fraser University. As well as being a fourth-generation Japanese Canadian, Yan was one of the first experts to use data to chart the flow of global capital. "It's opportunism, and it's a cover for the tremendous injustices that are emerging in the City of Vancouver and across the region."

Or, in the words of David Lam himself, quoted in a February, 1989 edition of the *Sun*: "When a Canadian is concerned about his own way of living, this concern is not racism."

Much like its insinuations of racial discrimination, the Laurier Report's conclusions about interprovincial migration have also proven demonstrably false. Ley, who has been studying the phenomenon for decades, conducted an extensive analysis of housing and immigration data, and concluded that the rise in Vancouver's home prices rose and fell in lockstep with the movement of wealthy Hong Kong immigrants. Rising until 1996, they subsequently declined at the same time as the collapse of the Hang Seng stock exchange, as investors attempted to liquidate their assets. Like the American investors of the 1950s, and the English investors of the 1970s, Asia's most affluent citizens have spent decades using Vancouver real estate as a means to export capital from a difficult market. And, like the Smithe government of the 1900s, the province and local real estate interests were more than willing to accommodate them, in hopes of filling their coffers and stimulating the economy. And the resulting spike in prices has affected lower-and-middle-income Canadians of all ethnicities.

As of 2019, allegations of racism are still regularly deployed in debates about real estate, and this is in part because many of the individuals who first advanced it in the public discourse have gone on to become even more intimately involved with the real estate industry. The *Sun*'s Jamie Lamb later took a job with consulting firm Northwest Public Affairs, penning editorials on behalf of corporate clients like the BC Liberal Party, and the oil and gas industry.

"Northwest Public Affairs often uses newspaper opinion and commentary pages to help clients tell their stories," reads the company's website, "writing articles for clients that build awareness of, and support for, their issues. And when the firm's principals find an issue that's personally interesting or compelling, they'll write op-eds and commentaries under their own names."

David Baxter, the study's lead author, would later found the Urban Futures Institute, which, after years of conducting research for Rennie Marketing Systems (one of the city's most prominent overseas real estate marketing companies), would be absorbed into the company's "Intelligence Division" in 2017.

After stepping down as dean of the Sauder School of Business, Michael Goldberg authored a series of additional studies for the Laurier Institution, and went on to become a regular source for local newspapers reporting on the impact of global capital on Vancouver's housing market. Usually cited as an impartial expert, his deep and ongoing connections to the real estate industry are never disclosed.

"Metro Vancouver's real estate market is now a dystopian tableau of panic buying, tax fraud, property flipping, overseas pre-construction condominium sales, stone cold speculation and elaborate, multiple-account money transfer rigmaroles that are the conduit of choice for drug cartel tycoon," wrote *Maclean's* in February of 2018. "Not even the heaviest regulatory hands at the controls of the Chinese Communist Party's surveillance state seem capable of shutting the networks down."

But the industry couldn't operate in a vacuum; they were eagerly abetted by the civic and provincial governments who, like the Smithe Conservatives before them, threw their doors open wide to global capital, with few strings attached.

And nobody epitomized this approach better than one man.

His name was Gordon Campbell, and he was about to be the best friend the development industry ever had.

20.

THE COUP

"The question is, how do we preserve our neighbourhoods?"

— City Councillor Gordon Campbell, October, 1985

AFTER TWENTY YEARS on city council, Harry Rankin was running for mayor.

He had always been a political oddball — cantankerous, combative, and opinionated (and, it should be noted, sexist), often the sole dissenting voice in a city hall that had, for decades, been dominated by NPA aldermen. He had made no secret of his communist leanings, and over the years, had always been a champion of workers' rights and social justice — both as a lawyer and on city council — having worked to set up BC's Legal Aid Society, and defending low-income and Indigenous clients (including going toe-to-toe with the RCMP on behalf of deceased Tsilcot'in Elder Fred Quilt). The indefatigable Rankin had campaigned twelve times before being elected in 1966, and now, with the sale of the Expo lands in the rear-view mirror, and the civic election ramping up, polls showed he was the clear front runner to lead the city.

His opponent was a one-term councillor and marginally successful housing developer named Gordon Campbell.

The two men couldn't have been more different.

Hailing from Point Grey, Campbell had first won his seat as an NPA alderman in 1984, and during his first few interviews with local newspapers, he came out as an enthusiastic supporter of the development community.

"The only way we're going to change the city is to get private investment to do the things that the council wants them to do," he said. "As a developer, I'm involved in creating jobs, trying to meet the city's objectives and I think we've lost sight of the fact that the development community can be a positive contributor both to jobs and making the city a better place."

When asked if his involvement with developers might constitute a conflict of interest at city hall, Campbell scoffed, saying claims of that nature came "from people who do not recognize the goals of the development community." But in truth, his ties to the industry ran deep. Having taken his first job on a Daon Developments' construction site as a teenager, Campbell went on to become the executive assistant to TEAM Mayor Art Phillips in the early 1970s. During that time, he was given a crash course in how public resources could subsidize private enterprise; shortly after council rezoned the False Creek industrial lands owned by Marathon Realty in 1973, Campbell suddenly left city hall to take a job with the company as a development officer, meaning that, in the words of SFU housing expert and historian Donald Gutstein: "He was responsible for rezoned lands the city had rezoned while he was working for Phillips."

After the market crash of the 1980s, developing the False Creek lands became unfeasible, but thanks to the intimate connections between Marathon and the government, the company still managed to turn a substantial profit.

"The Bill Bennett government conveniently came forward with plans for a stadium," Gutstein later wrote. "Campbell was all smiles when he announced that Marathon would be glad to sell the land to the province at a good price. It was still worth three times as much as its value before the city rezoning."

In 1981, armed with inside knowledge of the stadium's location, Campbell started his own development company (Citycore), eventually building a hotel known as the Georgian Court in the neighbourhood. It immediately began hemorrhaging money — between 1988 and 1993, it lost more than $2.9 million — and by 1986, the year Campbell threw his hat in the electoral ring, Citycore owed the city of Vancouver $888,745 in property taxes.

While he had been initially unashamed of his development background, Campbell quickly changed his tune; when, during a council meeting in early 1985, councillors Bruce Ericken and Libby Davies wondered aloud how much money Campbell had taken from Marathon and other developers, Campbell remained conspicuously silent. And this change in his rhetoric coincided with the reinvention of the party he had come to represent: the NPA.

After losing the civic dominance it had enjoyed for decades, the party was in chaos.

Recognizing the left-of-centre nature of council at the time, and the voting preferences of Vancouverites, the NPA realized, if it were to have any hope of victory, it would have to change its image, remaking itself in the eyes of voters as more than simply a free-enterprise party in the pockets of big developers. In recent elections, the NPA had gained no ground, and even lost their majority on the school board, as various factions vied for control of the party's future. In 1985, there was an attempted coup on the board of directors; their initial choice for mayoral candidate in the 1986 election was George Puil, who represented the NPA's old guard, and who, according to internal polling, stood no chance against Rankin.

So, in advance of the election, the party rebranded.

And among the chief architects of this rebrand was Brian Calder. In the years since his initial stint on council, Calder had moved into the real estate game, and established himself as the NPA's president — a useful position for someone in the development community. And in November of 1985, under Calder's direction, the party unveiled its new image, and its new candidate for mayor: Gordon Campbell. Abruptly, talk of development and developers was pushed below the surface, and Campbell, with his broad grin and can-do newspaper quotes, was put front and centre.

"Certain members of council have tried to label the NPA of today with a developer mentality and a freeway mentality," Calder noted, in the *Sun*, "which isn't there at all."

Mayoral candidates Gordon Campbell and Harry Rankin kissing babies for a Vancouver Centennial photo-op, October 6, 1986 (CVA AM1576-S6-12-F52). Photo by Glen Erickson. Copyright COV.

However, when asked at a press conference how much of his campaign was being funded by developers, Campbell dodged the question. But when it came to housing, his voting record demonstrated that his priorities were firmly in line with development community. Before he had even been elected as an alderman, he was quoted in the newspapers advocating for certain Champlain Heights housing cooperatives to be sold to developers, and the money used to relocate the residents. When Mayor Mike Harcourt went to Victoria, asking for special measures to prevent Downtown East Side residents from facing rent increases or evictions during Expo '86, Campbell, along with other NPA councillors, voted against the measure (many such evictions were eventually carried out, leading to several deaths). He also repeatedly spoke out in favour of cracking down on secondary suites, a way for cash-strapped locals to subsidize their mortgages — claiming at one point that if developers weren't allowed to rezone a neighbourhood, residents shouldn't be allowed to, either.

Nonetheless, as the election neared, the gap between Campbell and Rankin began to narrow.

While both sides had publicly declared a campaign budget of three hundred thousand dollars (the maximum allowed), the NPA spent at least one hundred thousand dollars more than that (with Rankin claiming it was closer to one million), most of it on TV ads. Immediately, there were calls from COPE for Campbell to disclose his donors. But, as there were no laws in place to require it at the civic level, Campbell declined (according to an independent *Sun* investigation, eighty per cent of the NPA's cash was raised at fundraising dinners for the business elite). And when questioned, Campbell promised he wouldn't take part in any council decisions that would be potential conflicts of interest — either for himself, or his supporters.

In the months that followed, the candidates squared off over a variety of issues, but few were more contentious than Vancouver's future relationship with land developers. In this, Campbell and Rankin were diametrically opposed, with Rankin advocating for strict controls on global capital in the real estate market.

"The basic issue is to give Canadians the first and only chance to buy," he later said, "that means Canadian residents or landed immigrants. No offshore people should be allowed to speculate in this market."

The election was a contentious one. The NPA offices were defaced, and at one point Campbell even received death threats — albeit indirectly — in the form of graffiti reading "Kill Gordon Campbell, Give The City A Chance" spray-painted on a Point Grey mailbox. But in the end, Rankin's solid lead, and decade of experience were no match for the NPA machine; the party scored its biggest electoral win in sixty years, thanks in large part to development money.

"They [developers] packaged him and sold him," Rankin said, bitterly, in the pages of the *Sun*, "and I'm not going to congratulate him for being packaged and sold like a piece of beef."

"It's been 15 years since we had a developer in control of council and a lot of people are forgetting what it was like," noted SFU Professor Donald Gutstein. "Developers want so much from city hall. They want to be able to tear down buildings, lower taxes on commercial and industrial buildings. They want to get the city out of all these social programs because they don't want their tax dollars to finance them."

"There will," Rankin warned, "be special rules for their developer friends who are waiting to carve this city up."

And indeed there were.

Campbell's personal friend Jim Moodie (who ran Moodie Consultants, and also worked for Marathon Realty, as well as lending a hand at NPA fundraising dinners) was awarded $2.4 million in city contracts between 1987 and 1993 — including a 1993 contract for $203,000, approved in a secret session of city council. While Moodie had received city contracts before, the dollar amounts rose sharply after Campbell took power, and began to include opaque line items like "Professional Services." As for the Georgian Court Hotel, Campbell retained his shares until 1987 (despite claims of having divested himself of them in 1984), and two members of his family — his brother Michael, and father-in-law Fred Chipperfield — held onto theirs into the 1990s. From his position on council, Campbell campaigned for the Downtown Stadium for Vancouver Committee, which was, by no small coincidence, set to be built across from the Georgian Court. During the same period, the city gave the stadium's developers a a number of sweet deals, exempting them from getting a development permit, and giving out a forty thousand dollar subsidy for fast-tracking the project.

After helping get Campbell elected, Brian Calder recommitted himself full-time to real estate; in addition to serving as the head of his own company, he also became head of the Real Estate Board of Greater Vancouver.

And before the end of the 1990s, his friendship with Campbell would yield huge dividends.

As for Campbell himself, he went on to serve three successive terms as Vancouver's mayor, trouncing a string of left-wing candidates including Jean Swanson, and Downtown East Side advocate Jim Green in a series of elections that were, curiously, fought in large part on issues of housing affordability. Taking a page from the Laurier Institution's playbook, NPA victories often involved co-opting the media and academics-for-hire (Campbell's narrow victory over Green in 1990 was, in part, the result of *Future Growth, Future Shock,* a study published in the *Vancouver Sun* by two UBC academics who admitted, in 2004, that they had been bought off by the development industry as part of a "calculated attempt to change an ideology"). Under Campbell, the Vancouver NPA spent four times as much on the 1990 election campaign as their political opponents, with much of that money coming from wealthy donors; by 1990, Campbell was hosting two annual fundraising dinners per year, with prominent members of the real estate community buying entire tables, including Concord Pacific, Victor Li, Jack Poole, Century 21 founder Peter Thomas, and Brian Calder (a fundraising dinner in 1990 brought in one hundred thousand dollars in a single night).

"It's the developers," complained Bruce Yorke, then the treasurer for COPE. "There's an obvious difference in wealth between their supporters and ours."

Although defeated, Harry Rankin continued to serve as a city councillor until 1993.

After his retirement, COPE virtually disappeared from the political landscape, unable to elect a single candidate between 1996-1999. However, with the candidacy of Larry Campbell (later fictionalized as Dominic Da Vinci in the CBC series *Da Vinci's Inquest*), the party experienced a brief resurgence, before a portion of its candidates (including Jim Green) moved on to form Vision Vancouver. But the election of Gordon Campbell and the return of the NPA to civic dominance was a watershed moment for the City of Vancouver, the final link in a chain that had begun with David Lam, and continued through the implementation of the Pacific Strategy and the sale of the Expo Lands to Li Ka-Shing.

It was over.

Developer interests would be behind the wheel — first civically, and then, with Campbell's election as premier, provincially — for the next fourteen years. And their gain would be everyone else's loss.

21.
CONCERT

"What sort of economy and society will there be if only the very rich can afford to live here? Current high housing prices have definite economic growth and job creation implications for the province. If high-priced executives can't afford to move here, how can lesser-paid people afford to stay?"

— *The Vancouver Province*, 1981

"THERE WILL NOT BE any conflict between what Brian Calder is doing and what I am," NPA mayoral hopeful Gordon Campbell told reporters in 1986, "and if there is, I would step down from it. Brian Calder is not going to come to me and say: 'Please rezone my property because it's going to triple in value.'"

Less than three years later, Campbell did something very much like that, using his position as mayor to unilaterally let Calder and a group of real estate insiders in on the deal of a lifetime. It was May of

1989, and the city was, once again, in the midst of a rental vacancy crisis. Although the Campbell-led council crowed about having presided over the largest number of housing starts in city history, less than ten per cent of those were rentals. In 1989, only six hundred units were built in total. Without provincial rent control (axed by the Social Credit government in the early 1980s), rents had skyrocketed, and a slew of demolitions in Kerrisdale and Kitsilano led experts to urge for a temporary demolition freeze. To grapple with the problem, the city hosted a day-long housing symposium in May of 1989, resulting in more than twenty different resolutions to be presented to council. But Campbell had other ideas.

And two weeks later, he unveiled his plan:

The city would give approximately fifty million dollars worth of land at the foot of the Granville Street bridge to a consortium of private developers, in hopes of stimulating the construction of affordable housing. Funded in part by private investment, and in part by union pension funds, the city would grant eighty-year leases on the land, in exchange for the construction of two thousand affordable units by 1990, and two thousand more for every year thereafter. In exchange for the land, the company would pay the city seventy-five per cent of their net operating income (after operating expenses and financing costs). The project, in Campbell's words, would be "privately-built housing with a social conscience."

"It will not be social housing," Campbell noted, "and it will not be condominiums in disguise."

There was no public tender process. No bids were solicited.

And the consortium lucky enough to receive the city's generosity included Brian Calder, David Podmore, and Jack Poole. Poole and Campbell had grown close over the years (to the point where Poole was referred to in the media as a "bagman" for the Campbell-led provincial Liberal Party), and the idea was, in part, Poole's attempt to stage a comeback after the disastrous implosion of Daon Developments. In what was perhaps a tip of the hat to David Oppenheimer, Poole named the consortium the "Vancouver Land Corporation", putting in $750,000 of his own money, and raising the remaining twenty-eight million dollars through union pension funds, with the help of BC Federation of Labour president Ken Georgetti (also on the VLC's board of directors). While Calder had once been quoted as saying that he preferred a society with "as little government intervention as possible," he didn't seem to mind government aid when it was subsidizing his business operations; in fact, the company wasn't coy about its future intentions, with its prospectus noting that city land was only a starting point, with the final goal being "to expand the types of properties in which it invests, as well as the geographic areas in which these investments are made."

Following the announcement, Campbell's opponents were furious.

"It is a reflection of the way the mayor does his business," fumed councillor Libby Davies, "and that is, he cooks up this political agenda behind closed doors and then he unveils it and says: 'There it is, and I'm shoving it through.'"

Both councillor Harry Rankin and The Tenants Rights Council criticized the deal for putting public money in the pockets of private developers without any consultation — a sentiment echoed by COPE's Jim Green.

"I went through the position paper," Green noted, "and I see at least three levels of government subsidy going into private housing, and I don't like it."

While Campbell insisted it wouldn't cost taxpayers a dime, the program would in fact be subsidized by taxpayers, through the $6.7 million of taxpayer cash allocated through BC's Rental Supply Program, and at least $7.5 million from the city's Property Endowment Fund (revenue from city-owned land, ostensibly a public resource). To make things worse, nothing in the company's prospectus kept it tied to building affordable rental housing, and Poole himself was open about the VLC's plans, noting, in the *Sun*: "We won't be con-centrating on city-owned land. But we'll be looking for a jump-start from it."

Before the development could officially proceed, a vote would need to be taken in city council. But by 1989, council was controlled by the Campbell-led NPA, and the motion easily passed in August, with councillors voting along predictable party lines.

That is, except for Jonathan Baker; Baker, then considered the logical successor to Gordon Campbell, instead broke rank with his fellow NPA councillors, and took a high-profile stand against his boss and the VLC.

"I told them we can't go ahead with this," he explained, in an interview with the *Sun*. "This was public money and you're giving $50 million of land to one developer without public tender and there is no valid public purpose. I thought it was going to be the big-gest municipal scandal that ever occurred. But it wasn't."

In addition to being a municipal lawyer, Baker had worked as a social planner at city hall during the 1970s, contributing to projects like the Vancouver East Cultural Centre, the Granville Mall, and Granville Island. He had also run unsuccessfully as the NPA's mayo-ral candidate in 1982. Throughout the spring of 1990, Campbell and Baker waged a war of words in the press, and for his disobedience, Baker was excommunicated from the NPA.

And while a full-fledged scandal never materialized, public out-rage at the VLC deal extended well beyond Baker. In fact, in the fall of 1990, Vice President David Podmore took out nearly a full page in the *Sun*'s op-ed section to complain about the company's shoddy treatment in the press.

By 1990, the VLC was admitting that rents would be higher than expected, citing high land prices and building costs. The rental units would also be tiny; one VLC project, at 600 Drake Street, would fea-ture 191 "microsuites," ranging from 280–400 square feet (by contrast, bachelor suites in Daon Developments' Anchor Pointe, located nearby, were 450 square feet).

In the end, less than twelve hundred units were ever built on city land. And they weren't particularly affordable; in fact, studios and one-bedroom suites at The Drake rented at rates comparable to — and often above — market rates.

"It's been a huge winner," Georgetti beamed, in 2010. "Everyone got what was expected. We got a good company that has produced hundreds of thousands of hours of union work. And we're making good money for retired people all over BC."

But in a 2002 story for *Monday Magazine*, journalist Russ Francis had a different opinion.

"In exchange for access to forty-eight million dollars worth of public land, VLC promised to build up to two thousand units of 'affordable housing' each year," Francis wrote. "But they only ever built 1,143 units, total. And not one of the units was 'affordable,' according to any meaning of the word that I'm aware of. In a report to shareholders, VLC boasted that the rent for all of the units was higher than that in nearby buildings."

And, true to his word, Poole and his associates used these initial projects as a chance to expand, leaving any claims of affordable housing far behind them; in 1992, the company reorganized, focusing on property management, and market-rate housing for mid-income earners. By 1994, they were in the casino game, working to develop a facility on the False Creek waterfront. In a 1994 interview, the VLC's president of finance admitted that the company's social purpose had become "kind of vague."

The Vancouver Land Corporation would go on to change its name to Concert Properties, and today the company — which is still funded in part by union pensions — deals in market condos, commercial property, and seniors' living. They have a portfolio of more than 7,600 properties, and assets in excess of $1.4 billion.

As of 1994, the company had paid the city just twenty-eight thousand dollars in lease rates on land worth twenty-eight million dollars.

INTERLUDE:
A Brief History of Bob Rennie

Bob Rennie was selling a house per day before he graduated high school — although only in the technical sense. Having dropped out just three months before graduation, he wasn't awarded his diploma until 2006, well after he had established himself as Vancouver's "Condo King" (a title he personally despises), and the real estate industry's most high-profile face. Having grown up on the East Side in a working-class family, Rennie began to consider real estate as a career at seventeen, after seeing an appraiser come to his childhood home to evaluate its worth. He got his real estate license at nineteen, and by the time he was in his thirties, he was one of the region's most successful realtors, selling, on average, one home every single day.

"I've been doing this for 28 years," Rennie later told the *Sun*. "Let's face it, I don't know how to do anything else. When I was 19, it was either become a bartender, or a realtor. Thankfully, I guess I made the right choice."

One of Rennie's early secrets to success was that he, taking a page from David Lam's book, would faciliate every aspect of a real estate transaction; Rennie would buy a sixty-foot lot, sell it to a developer (who would build homes, which Rennie would also subsequently sell), and to maximize his own returns, he would also assist buyers in selling their existing homes. But following the sale of the Expo Lands to Li Ka-Shing, Rennie had begun refining his approach even further, using a concept that Concord Pacific had introduced to the Canadian market, and which would become his signature: condominium pre-sales. Before Concord Pacific's debut on the scene, pre-sales were unusual in Canada. But in Rennie's hands, they became a multi-billion-dollar industry, catering largely to overseas buyers, where returns would be substantially higher. Before the 1990s, Rennie had never sold condominiums. By 1992, he and then-partner Dan Ulinder (who had introduced him to the condo game) made headlines when they sold 189 suites in a building at 1189 Howe Street in just four hours. By the late 1990s, Rennie was Metro Vancouver's most successful salesman, with a personal record of $127 million in condo sales in 1996 alone. The following year, Rennie bought out Ulinder, and Rennie Marketing Systems was born.

By the end of the millennium, he had — or was in the process of cultivating — a long list of powerful friends: Gordon Campbell, Rich Coleman, and former Mayor Gregor Robertson. Notable among these friends was City Planner Larry Beasley; chummy throughout Rennie's rise to prominence, the two took long walks together (often weekly), to discuss the future of the city. When he was tapped to help sell the controversial Woodward's development in the Downtown East Side, Rennie again made headlines when he did it in a single day — although more than half of the suites sold went to investors rather than residents.

"In Vancouver, this merging of the public and private sector to do things is so much more advanced than in many cities," said

Beasley, who would go on to call Rennie a "social broker," "And he's one of the most important players."

And as his fortune grew, Rennie became even more important. By the mid-2000s, he was, in many ways, running the show; not only did he serve as the chief fundraiser for the governing Liberal Party (in power for more than fifteen years), he was also a fundraiser — and the largest individual donor — to civic juggernaut Vision Vancouver. The condo projects he went on to market were among the largest and most opulent in Vancouver — most of them marketed and sold to overseas buyers. He has also become a common target of scorn and derision for his role in the city's ongoing affordability crisis; after the industry spent years downplaying the role of global investment in the local market, public demand began mounting for the introduction of a Foreign Buyer Tax in 2015, until pressure from the industry — and Rennie in particular — managed to delay the initiative for another two years. In 2016, Rennie's status as a political insider was readily apparent, when he let slip that he knew about the upcoming introduction of the tax three weeks before the public did.

"Three weeks ago, I knew there was going to be a tax on foreign ownership," he told *Globe and Mail* journalist Mike Hager. "I didn't know it would be 15 per cent, I thought it would be five to eight percent. All the polling showed people were frantic and wanted a tax on foreign ownership."

He has also come under fire for selling entire developments to his wealthy friends — including The Ellsworth, and 8X On The Park, before marketing the units to the public (in the Woodward's development, Rennie's company purchased three entire floors).

"Mr. Rennie said developers advertise to the public as a sort of fallback policy," explained a 2016 article by *The Globe and Mail*'s Kathy Tomlinson, "If the insiders who get first dibs do not buy enough units, they can sell what is left to the next tier of interested buyers"(it should be noted that this practice is widespread within the industry, and that many of these buyers are speculators with no intention of living on the property, who would instead use the practice of contract assignment, or "shadow flipping" to sell the unit before the sale closed).

Six months after the Foreign Buyer Tax story saw print, Rennie stepped down in an official capacity as the Liberals' chief fundraiser. In the election that followed, the party was defeated at the polls, and many members of the real estate industry shifted their allegiances to the governing NDP.

In 2006, Bob Rennie finally received his high school diploma.

Two years later, he was given an honorary doctorate from the Emily Carr Institute of Art and Design (to which he has been a major charitable donor). As of 2019, he owns one of the largest contemporary art collections in Canada, and Rennie Marketing Systems boasts annual profits that are in the billions of dollars.

"Everything this city has evolved into over the last 20 years," former Vancouver Mayor Larry Campbell said, in 2008, "has Larry Beasley and Bob Rennie written all over it."

22.
RENT CONTROL (Part II)

"We are here today because we are angry at the indifference and lack of political will demonstrated by all levels of government and particularly our city council. This indifference has allowed the housing crisis to continue and worsen. We are here today because we believe there are solutions to the present housing crisis. The days of asking for your cooperation are over. We come here demanding that you take action. If you think this demonstration is noisy and loud, just wait a few months."

— Vancouver Community Housing Forum Brief, 1989

IN DECEMBER of 1989, more than one hundred people descended on city hall, carrying signs which read "Save Our Homes! Evict the Mayor!" and "Let Them Eat Condos!" Standing outside council chambers, they read a brief drafted by the Vancouver Community Housing Forum, while inside, Reverend Art Griffin of DERA asked for two minutes of silence, out of respect for "the victims of indecision and oppression from landlords." The protestors came from diverse economic circumstances; some were from the Downtown East Side. Some were apartment residents facing eviction. One was a homeowner in posh Point Grey, telling the media: "I'm here because of my conscience." The group demanded a moratorium on both demolitions and the closure of secondary suites, and the return of provincial rent control. When he took the floor, Mayor Gordon Campbell merely shrugged, saying: "I don't believe there is more that we can do." His government, he told protestors, had "done more than any previous council" (in reality, under Campbell, virtually no rental housing had been constructed in 1989).

He was roundly booed.

But the protestors' tactic worked; within weeks, Campbell had contacted the province, appealing to Housing Minister Peter Dueck in hopes of having them reinstate the long-defunct Rentalsman's Office. He also began to consult with other Lower Mainland mayors on the subject, and the city even briefly considered the idea of a civic rent review board.

In the years since the Social Credit government had scrapped provincial rent control, things had gotten ugly. Between 1984–1989, average rents for a one-bedroom apartment in Vancouver had increased by forty per cent, and for a two or three bedroom, it had grown by a staggering eighty per cent. And despite SoCred claims that deregulation would stimulate construction, apartment completions had all but stopped; in 1983, the final year of rent control, 750 apartments were built in Greater Vancouver. By 1988, after five years of no rent control, it was just 315.

"There's absolutely no profit to be made in developing rental properties now in Vancouver," complained Brian Calder, by then president of the Vancouver Real Estate Board. "There's too much risk, no rate of return, and government interference."

Due to the immense profits to be gleaned from condominium housing, the construction of purpose-built rentals had been flat for decades, and by 1990, the city's rental vacancy rate once again sat at 0.1%. By the 1990s, BC was the only province in Canada without rent control legislation in place, yet the mere mention of the measure had local real estate interests frothing at the mouth.

"Ontario hasn't had much success with rent review," scoffed Housing Minister Peter Dueck, "nor has anywhere else in the world" (In fact, Toronto, Vancouver's closest competitor, was using rent control quite effectively to keep rents in line with income).

"At a time when Eastern Europeans are struggling to free themselves from the economic tyranny of socialism," opined Fraser Institute toady Walter Block, "it would be the height of folly for us to adopt such central planning as rent control."

Added Calder: "It's no mere coincidence that the cities in North America with the largest number of homeless are also the cities with rent controls."

This was fundamentally untrue.

Then, in the summer of 1990, UBC's Centre for Human Settlements released a damning study on the abolition of rent control, finding that removing provincial regulations had no measurable effect on increasing housing supply.

"We have done a 20-year run on the numbers on housing starts and conditions, looking for relations between the lifting of controls and starts, and we have found none," director David Hulchanski said, in an interview. "All the quotes from government officials and politicians about what would happen when controls came off — none of it came true. All that happened was that rents went up."

As public discussion intensified, landlords began to get skittish. Then, in 1991, former Vancouver Mayor Mike Harcourt led the provincial NDP to victory, and, fearful that the new left-of-centre government would reimpose rent controls, at least a dozen landlords hiked their rents by twenty-five to thirty per cent. North Vancouver residents were especially hard-hit, with landlords increasing rents by thirty to sixty per cent. In some cases, the increases were tied to a rebate program, but this was a diversionary tactic — rebates were voluntary, and owners could revoke the rebate at any time.

"It's like an antidote," claimed David Goodman of Block Brothers Realty. "It's being done by sophisticated, tuned-in landlords who don't want to get caught with their pants down."

Tenants weren't impressed.

By 1993, approximately sixty per cent of the city's population was renting, and rents had already increased by forty per cent between 1987 and 1994. In Vancouver, annual rent increases were over ten times higher than in any other city in Canada. In December of 1992, as part of a campaign led by the Tenants Rights Action Coalition, provincial Labor Minister Moe Sihota was besieged with more than two thousand letters pleading for the reinstatement of rent control. TRAC staged other protest actions, including "Tenant Survival Day," a park party aimed at raising awareness by featuring rental horror stories, and giving out awards for those who had suffered the year's worst landlord abuses. Rent controls were a major talking point during the 1993 civic election, with COPE and the NPA assuming their familiar positions — for and against, respectively. But despite the fears of property owners, the Harcourt-led NDP steered clear of rent control, with Housing Minister Joan Smallwood instead establishing a dispute-resolution system to protect tenants against unjustifiable rent increases or sudden eviction.

"These changes are aimed at people who do not act responsibly or who abuse the rights of others," Smallwood said. "The system is market-sensitive, and relates to the situation of each individual landlord. For the first time since the abolition of the rentalsman 15 years ago, tenants have the right to approach a third party to deal with exorbitant rent increases."

The real estate industry was apoplectic.

"This appalling piece of legislation represents a major intrusion into the marketplace, supposedly on behalf of tenants hit by high rent increases," read an anonymous editorial in the pages of the *Sun*. "But in reality it will be damaging to them. What tenants need is choice, so that they can thumb their noses at gouging landlords and move to other digs."

Facing off against TRAC was the Rental Housing Council of BC, which claimed to represent more than forty-five hundred apartment owners. The bill, the RHC complained, was rent control in disguise, an interventionist measure in a rental market that was healthy (the group claimed the city's rental vacancy rate was three per cent, when in fact it was much lower), and capable of policing itself.

"Say No! To A Dumb Idea", the RHC wrote, taking out a half-page ad in the *Sun*. "The government is doing enough to make your life miserable with high taxes and skitterish [sic] interest rates. You don't need red tape and rent control to now rob the little break from your mortgage-helper suite."

While secondary suites were still technically illegal, the city had adopted a much more relaxed attitude toward them in the years since the emergence of the Vancouver Special. In 2007, they were finally legalized, providing a desperately-needed bump in the city's housing supply (as of 2019, secondary housing like basement suites accounts for roughly half of all rental stock). And in the meantime, TRAC and other advocacy groups kept pushing. Rent control, they argued, should be tied to units rather than tenants, and rent increases pegged to inflation. They also argued in favour of making landlords responsible for repairs.

"Human rights are essentially a bundle of rights entirely removed from the domain of the market," noted David Hulchanski, author of the 1991 UBC study on rent control. "Security of tenure and rent regulations have been instituted as a means of counteracting the influence of private market power over a basic human need: shelter."

BC had been without any form of rent control for nearly twenty years by the time the Liberal government of Gordon Campbell finally amended the Residential Tenancy Act in the summer of 2003. After decades of making a clamour, the real estate industry remained curiously quiet on the bill, likely because its terms were so generous to property owners; unlike in other jurisdictions, BC's landlords could increase rent by three to four per cent above the Consumer Price Index, and rent controls were tied to tenants rather than the units themselves (a provision readily abused by property owners, who would use minor renovations as an excuse to evict tenants and subsequently increase the rent).

At first, landlords could defer increases for up to three years — something ultimately omitted from the final legislation after strenuous protest from advocacy groups, and from Vancouver Mayor Larry Campbell. Otherwise, the bill drew very little media coverage at all, outside of Rental Owners and Managers Association head Al Kemp assuring a *Sun* journalist that "he doubts landlords would ever raise rents by the maximum amount, and said the rental market would dictate prices. No landlord would be willing to lose a good renter for the prospect of a few dollars more."

Despite its overtly generous provisions for landlords, the updated Residential Tenancy Act did represent a small victory for affordability. It would be one of the few. Tenancy legislation remained untouched for more than fifteen years, until, in 2018, faced with an unprecedented housing crisis, the NDP government of John Horgan imposed stricter rent controls; like in other jurisdictions, rent increases were finally pegged to inflation, fines for wrongful evictions were increased, and a "geographic increase" clause was removed, which allowed landlords to substantially increase rent to correspond with other buildings in the same area. TRAC still exists, providing legal education about tenant rights, and even direct advocacy, alongside groups like the Vancouver Tenant's Union (the same Vancouver Tenants Union started by Bruce Yorke in the 1970s), and in 2017, Vancouver elected its first long-term renter as Mayor — independent candidate Kennedy Stewart.

As of 2019, Vancouver's rental vacancy rate sits at 0.8%, and the debate over rent control is ongoing.

"There is a huge segment of the population for which the private market is just never going to meet their housing needs," current VTU spokesperson Liam McClure said, in an interview with the *Sun*. "As long as Vancouver's been a city, there's been housing crises."

COMPLETION

*"We live in the land of destiny. In the land of
wealth where, though gold is not idly picked off
the rocks or from the pavements in the streets,
it is just as surely gained from the platted acres
and twenty-footers around us. One day an
artisan may put the scanty savings of a lifetime
into a tiny holding out among the evergreens,
and on the morrow almost, he is building city
blocks from the proceeds thereof."*

— R.J. McDougall, *BC Magazine*, 1911

IN THE SPRING of 2002, a sixty-nine-year-old Jack Poole stood before a roomful of developers.

"If the Olympic bid wasn't happening," he told the crowd, "we would have to invent something."

Recently, Poole had been appointed head of the Vancouver Olympic Committee by his longtime friend, Premier Gordon Campbell, and following his speech, the excitement in the room was palpable. As Expo '86 had proven, place marketing was a boon for the real estate industry, and there was no better piece of place marketing than

the Olympic Games. It was a speculative investment in the future —
specifically, the future of the industry's balance sheet. And, as usual, it
would be paid for with public funds.

"At the risk of sounding naive, we had understood the bid was
aimed at getting the Games," wrote *Western Investor* editor Frank
O'Brien, who witnessed the meeting, "raising Vancouver's international profile and welcoming elite athletes to one of the world's best
skiing locations. Wrong. The real purpose of the 2010 Olympic bid is
to seduce the provincial and federal governments and long-suffering
taxpayers into footing a billion-dollar bill to pave the path for future
real estate sales."

The process would closely mirror that of Expo, and included
many of the same players — most of whom represented real estate
interests; among the board of directors for the bid corporation were
David Podmore (Poole's partner at Concert Properties), Concord
Pacific, Canaccord's Peter Brown, real estate giant David McLean,
Stanley Kwok (former vice president of Concord Pacific), and
Robert Fung (director of Gordon Capital, a firm owned by Li Ka-
Shing's son Richard). In time for the 2003 civic referendum on the
subject, condo marketer Bob Rennie purchased sixteen full-page ads
in both the *Sun* and the *Province*, supporting the "Yes" side.

"This isn't about an 18-day Olympic experience," beamed chairman Arthur Griffiths. "This Olympics is all about a catalyst for
change and a showcase for the world."

Plenty had already changed over the past ten years, since former
Vancouver Mayor Gordon Campbell had taken the helm of the
floundering BC Liberal Party (reducing the once-mighty NDP to just
two seats) back in 2001. His decade as premier was an unmitigated
disaster for affordability, coinciding with the largest spike in the
price of detached homes in Vancouver's history, as the government
threw open its doors to global capital with a total absence of regulatory oversight. Over the course of Campbell's tenure, the average

cost of a detached home in Vancouver soared — from just under four hundred thousand dollars in 2001 to almost two million dollars by 2016. During the same period, average apartment prices more than doubled. Over just five months in 2016, the price of homes rose by as much as they had between 1981 and 2005. While crowding out a generation of working Vancouverites, BC's housing market quickly became a haven for not just wealthy investors, but the global criminal elite, who used it to launder the proceeds of the drug trade (particularly fentanyl, which has since killed thousands of people in the Downtown East Side), and get around the capital controls imposed by the Chinese Communist Party. In 2018, an estimated five billion dollars in illegal money was laundered through BC's housing market, and the practice had become so widespread, that it became known internationally as the "Vancouver Model." The entire region's economy had become path-dependent, with even ancillary business activities being pulled into the real estate industry's orbit.

And politicians at both the civic and provincial level reaped the financial rewards.

In 2015, as nearly ten billion dollars worth of global capital poured into Vancouver's real estate market (one-third of the annual total), the real estate sector contributed more than a billion dollars in property transfer taxes to government coffers, as well as making more than ten million dollars in donations to the BC Liberal Party — more than twice as much as the other two largest industry contributors (mining and forestry). Meanwhile, many of the homes and apartments purchased in Vancouver remained empty. In posh Coal Harbour, a well-known repository for investment capital, a study conducted by SFU's Andy Yan estimated that approximately twenty-five per cent of condominiums were sitting vacant. As of 2019, non-resident ownership accounts for twenty per cent of condos citywide.

"Nobody wants to admit it," Rennie shrugged, in a 2010 interview with *La Presse*, on a trend he helped perpetuate, "but Vancouver has become a resort city where rich foreigners live a few months per year." The Games, he added, somewhat smugly, were a "$6-billion ad buy."

In 2007, as the Olympics drew near, Jack Poole was diagnosed with pancreatic cancer. As his condition worsened, newspapers and magazines featured glowing profiles of the longtime developer. *BC Business* chronicled his rags-to-riches (to rags, to riches) story, hailing him as a "a legendary builder and businessman." A civic plaza was named in his honour.

"British Columbia and Canada have lost a great friend," Gordon Campbell said, in a media statement following Poole's death in 2009.

There was no mention of the public land leveraged, the incentives abused, the senior citizens displaced.

Canaccord Financial CEO Peter Brown, the silver-spoon-wielding former head of the defunct Vancouver Stock Exchange, and one of the architects of the Expo Lands sale, was himself the subject of brief media adoration, after being awarded the Order of British Columbia in 2003. In addition to being part of the 2010 Bid Committee with Poole, he also went on to serve as chairman of the board at the Fraser Institute. Brown made the news in 2016 when he sold his thirty-one-million-dollar Point Grey mansion to a "student."

After returning to China, Victor Li assumed greater control of his father's business empire, running the conglomerate alongside Li Sr, who, now well into his eighties, still serves as company chairman. In 1996, Li was kidnapped by well-known gangster "Big Spender" Cheung Tze-Keung, and only released after his father paid a ransom of one billion dollars. Although a police report was never filed, "Big Spender" was subsequently executed in mainland China — amidst rumours of a deal between the elder Li and mainland authorities. As of 2010 the company, now known as CK Hutchison Holdings, boasted revenues of $4.2 billion.

After several scandals — including an arrest for drunk driving, and his resignation following the botched introduction of BC's har-

monized sales tax — Gordon Campbell was given a cushy appointment as Canada's high commissioner to the UK. As of 2019, he was
being investigated over allegations of sexual assault by a London
embassy worker.

The Olympic Games ultimately cost taxpayers seven billion dollars. And, as the 2010 Bid Committee had hoped, they were followed
by an immediate spike in home prices. Yet, subsequent studies found
that, outside of creating a windfall for the real estate and construction
industries, the Games had very limited economic benefit, leading to
no significant increase in tourist traffic, and no measurable improvement in Vancouver's international image. Unsurprisingly, a study
conducted out of the Sauder School of Business, under the direction
of Dean Emeritus Michael Goldberg claimed the opposite — that
the Games had, in fact, had no effect on city housing prices(little
mention was made of the fact that, like Goldberg, lead author Tsur
Somerville was bankrolled by the development industry; the Centre
for Urban Economics, which he founded, has a donors list that
includes Henderson Developments, Grosvenor, Polygon Homes,
and the Vancouver Home Builders' Association).

"We live in a land of destiny," R.J. MacDougall wrote, back in
1911. But as of this writing, that destiny is uncertain.

Concord Pacific, which owns one of the last available stretches of
undeveloped land on False Creek, is currently working with the City
of Vancouver on a plan to demolish the Georgia viaducts, thus opening up broad swathes of nearby real estate. Taxpayers will likely be
footing an outsize portion of the $1.7 billion bill. The company will
also reportedly pay to relocate the Vancouver Maritime Museum —
which sits on prime waterfront property in Kitsilano.

Following the retirement of CEO David Podmore, Concert Properties continues to announce new projects, including a comprehensive
redevelopment in West Coquitlam. The development is being billed as
"affordable."

Beginning in 2036, leases will begin to expire on the city-owned land in False Creek, leaving the fate of one of the region's most progressive housing developments unclear.

Luckily, the affordability crunch has helped to forge passionate advocates for housing justice, including SFU's Andy Yan and Josh Gordon, as well as Paul Kershaw of Generation Squeeze, former UBC researcher David Ley, the civic planning committee's Brandon Yan, and the group Housing Action for Local Taxpayers. The problem has also become one that politicians can no longer ignore. The BC Liberals fell in 2016, largely because of their role in the affordability crisis, and a perceived indifference to the plight of working Vancouverites. A coalition government between the NDP and the Green Party have since introduced a series of measures designed to reduce the inflow of global capital and cool the housing market, including taxes on both foreign buyers and empty homes — measures fought vigorously by the development industry. Because, although the greed of Vancouver's speculator and developer classes is worthy of the utmost contempt, the ultimate failure is a political one. The state of Vancouver real estate in 2019 is a policy disaster of the highest order, a sustained attempt to prop up the province's only profitable industry at the expense of everything else, a development borne of greed, idealogical blindness, and, at best, a profound ignorance about corruption and the workings of global capital. It isn't a new problem, but without appropriate and sustained public pressure, those in charge will continue with the same tired solutions (for example in 2019, Vancouver Mayor Kennedy Stewart announced a proposal for developer incentives to stimulate construction). Until the profit motive is removed or de-incentivized from certain portions of the housing market, and until the city, the province, and the federal government take steps to get involved (like in False Creek South), until non-market options are made viable, it will be business as usual. Learning from the past is often the best guide to the future.

And the past shows us that change of this magnitude is never presented from on high.

It has to be demanded.

Fought for.

Pushed on elected representatives through a campaign of steady pressure from below. Policy and regulation are profoundly unsexy words, but they are the only way forward. It it too late? It's hard to say. Path dependency may now be too entrenched to scale back without disaster.

And in the meantime the industry and its enablers will get away with whatever they can. Like they have for the past 130 years. They'll continue to sell to the highest bidder — even if that happens to be criminals or their powerful friends. They'll continue to flout rules and abuse incentives. They'll continue to claim the affordability crunch is the result of building costs or a lack of supply. They'll continue to co-opt debate using paid academics. They'll continue to deny, or shrug, or hide behind concepts like free enterprise or growth.

At least, they will as long as we let them.

Why should a piece of empty real estate be sacrosanct? Is the owner's right to keep it vacant superior to the right of local families to have a roof over their heads? Any public representative who answers "yes" to that question is not only out of sympathy with humanity but out of step with social progress. The choice is clear: to continue on the mindless drive toward a high-density prestige "executive city" — a Manhattan with mountains; or to redirect itself toward providing adequate housing and a decent environment. When the chips are down and people are suffering unnecessary exploitation, and a great many tenants are suffering unnecessary exploitation at the present time, a government isn't worth its salt if it doesn't stand up and protect that class of people. A great deal of time has been spent, by both public and private authorities, on analyzing the housing problem. We must now concentrate our efforts on finding the solution. Housing costs are high, but we can't afford to throw up our hands and say we can't afford to build many more houses until costs come down again. In a city growing as fast as ours this would be the counsel of stupidity and despair. We must have homes, and we must have them at prices people can afford to pay.

They said from the first the bubble would burst.

Because, before Vancouver became a city it was — first and foremost — a real estate investment.

Whether it remains that way is up to us.

ACKNOWLEDGEMENTS

Thanks to Mom and Dad, as always. Thanks to Caley and Kirsten for letting me crash on your couch and for listening to my yammering. Thanks to Brian Kaufman and Karen Green at Anvil Press for pushing this project, and for not having an immediate coronary over receiving a manuscript that was 20,000 words longer than it was supposed to be (oops). Thanks to Lani Russwurm for the newspapers.com hookup. DEAR GOD HOW DID WE DO ANY OF THIS BEFORE THE INTERNET?

Thanks to you, the reader, for acknowledging these acknowledgements, and taking a second to read them, even though they're stuffed at the very back of the book. I gratefully acknowledge your acknowledgement of these acknowledgements.

Thank you to caffeine, on which I'm currently soaring. Thank you to all of the researchers whose Masters and PhD theses I plundered for information. Thanks to Mike Harcourt and Karen O'Shannacery for taking my calls. A special shout-out to Andy Yan, Josh Gordon, Gary Mason, Kathy Tomlinson, Paul Kershaw, and all of the other journalists, analysts, and advocates who are out there every single day helping us work toward some measure of housing justice.

Thank you to the concept of language; when it comes to exploring the history of real estate, it's more effective than indistinct screaming.

Ms. Fortune: Thanks for playgrounds and Milkshake IPAs. You may be unlucky, but I'm fortunate to know you.

And finally, thanks to all the amazing, creative, inspiring humans I've met over the past eighteen months: Brian, Jeremy, Justina, James, Ash, Hilary, Gonz, little Ella, Kelly, Jess, the Jesses, Heather, Niki, Ala, Christina, Austin, and Justin.

We may not be able to afford houses, but you folks are my home.

Notes

Statistics on Vancouver's housing situation are largely taken from SFU Data Guru Andy Yan's online database, and from the text of Peter Germann's report on money laundering in the BC housing market.

GREEN

1: The Letter

Dating the meeting between Ross and Gravely is made possible by, among other things, an item in the May 29, 1884 edition of the *Manitoba Free Press* which states that A.W. Ross had headed west "with an eye to making some investments."

The letter regarding Ross' speculation practices was written by Deputy Minister of the Interior Alexander Mackinnon Burgess to Minister of the Interior Thomas White (1885).

W.E. Gravely's recollection of his meeting with Arthur Wellington Ross is taken from J.S. Matthews' *Early Vancouver* (Vol. 3, p. 183).

Information about Walter Gravely is taken from the Gravely Family Fonds — in particular his unfinished autobiography *Recollections of a Long Life* at the City of Vancouver Archives (hereafter CVA; Box: 512-E-03)

The *Manitoba Free Press'* assessment of Ross' character comes from the April 21, 1884 issue.

The two quotes from Alderman W.H. Gallagher come from J.S. Matthews' *Early Vancouver* (Vol. 1, p. 94).

The quotes from Ruth Morton are taken from J.S. Matthews' *Early Vancouver* (Vol. 5, p. 94).

2: The Syndicate

Walter Gravely's quote about the membership of the Coal Harbour Land Syndicate is taken from *Early Vancouver* (Vol. 3, p. 207).

The *Port Moody Gazette's* analysis of the Coal Harbour scheme is taken from the September 5, 1885 issue (p. 2).

James Hill's assessment of Coal Harbour comes from the Minnesota Historical Society, Great Northern Records, (J.J. Hill Correspondence and President Material, box 22.E.7.2F, file Angus, R.B., 1879-83, Hill to R.B. Angus, 10 February 1882).

Many of the details surrounding the provincial government's secret negotiations with the railway were furnished by Frank Leonard's excellent 'So Much Bumph: CPR Terminus Travails at Vancouver 1884–89' (*BC Studies* 166, Summer 2010).

H.P. McCraney's assessment of Oppenheimer and the land syndicate is taken from *Early Vancouver* (Vol. 1, p. 179).

W.C. Van Horne's letter to to A.W. Ross was written on September 17, 1884 (CVA; CPR papers).

An estimation of Postmaster Jonathan Miller's land holdings is taken from the 1891 Souvenir Edition of the *Vancouver Daily News-Advertiser*.

John Robson's purchase of lands near Coal Harbour is examined in the February 21, 1885 issue of the *Victoria Daily Colonist*, and Premier William Smithe's admission comes from the April 7, 1886 edition of the *Mainland Guardian*.

W.C. Van Horne's admission to Premier Smithe that he would take much less than the 4000+ hectares requested by the railroad comes from a September 9, 1884 letter (BC Archives 1885, Van Horne to Smithe, September 9, 1884; BC Archives, GR-1088, British Columbia, Department of Lands, file 77/85, Van Horne to Smithe, Private, September 9, 1884), and his willingness to grease the Premier's palm is demonstrated in a May 22, 1886 letter between W.C. Van Horne and Harry Abbott (Library and Archives Canada, M2259, Van Horne to H. Abbott, 22 May 1886).

The 1884 letter between W.C. Van Horne and A.B. Rogers can be found in Library and Archives Canada (Van Horne to Rogers, December 8, 1884, M2253).

An examination of W.E. Gravely's business practices, the speculative nature of his investments, and details of the Port Moody Swindle, are taken from Grant M. Longhurst's "Situate, lying, and being in the city of Vancouver': independent real estate entrepreneurs, 1884–1893', (MA Thesis, UBC, 1995)

Gravely's account of the arrest of Arthur Wellington Ross is taken from J.S. Matthews' *Early Vancouver* (vol 3, p. 208). Dating Ross' arrest is possible through Walter Gravely's transaction records, showing a conveyance of interest between Gravely, A.W. Ross, and other members of the Syndicate (CVA Gravely Family Fonds; Receipts; Box 512-E-03 fld 08)

3: Incorporation, Inc.

The Douglas Sladen quote at the top of the chapter, the piece about CPR attitudes, and Vancouver's designation as the "Constantinople of the West," are taken from *Frank Leslie's Popular Monthly* (Vol. 29, No. 5, December 1891).

Walter Gravely's account of the CPR land sale is taken from *Early Vancouver* (Vol. 4, p. 188).

Frank Hart's recollections are also taken from *Early Vancouve*r (Vol. 3, p. 226).

The letter referring to Jon Robson's success as a land speculator was written by Liberal MLA John Grant, and referenced in Patricia E. Roy's entry on Robson in the *Dictionary of Canadian Biography* (Vol. XII – 1891–1900). The estimate of Robson's assets at his death comes from the same source, but can't be entirely verified.

Assessments of the VLAIC's holdings are taken from the September 5, 1885 edition of the *Port Moody Gazette* (p. 2). Their holdings circa 1887 are taken from "The CPR and Vancouver's Development to 1900 (Norbert MacDonald, *BC Studies* 17, Spring 1973).

The value of city construction as of 1887 is taken from the 1888 edition of the *BC Directory*.

Details of Arthur Wellington Ross' life and death come from his obituary in the March 25, 1901 edition of the *Winnipeg Tribune* (p. 8).

4: The Park

The quote at the top of the chapter is from Hilda Glynn-Ward's shockingly racist *The Writing On The Wall* (1920; republished 1974 by University of Toronto Press).

The date of the survey crew's arrival at the Khatsahlano residence is an educated guess, made possible by referencing the Order-In-Council that granted Stanley Park to the City of Vancouver (June 8, 1887), and through Sean Kheraj's *Inventing Stanley Park* (UBC Press, 2013), which dates the commencement of road construction as October 1888. August Jack Khatsahlano's recollection of the incident is taken from *Early Vancouver*.

Estimates of the X̱wáy̱x̱way Big House's size, and Jonathan Miller's estimation of potlatch attendance comes from "Conversations with Khatsalano", p. 36 (CVA). J.S.Matthews' quote about X̱wáy̱x̱way also comes from "Conversations with Khatsalano", p. 23 A (CVA).

Archaeological evidence of the First Nations presence at X̱wáy̱x̱way and Chaythoos, and the quote about smallpox collected by Charles Hill-Tout, are both taken from *Inventing Stanley Park*.

The assessment of Col. Moody's land-grabbing activities is taken from F.W. Howay's "Early Settlement on Burrard Inlet" (*BC Historical Quarterly* 1, 2; 1937). The text of Robert Burnaby's letter to his brother comes from *Land of Promise: Robert Burnaby's Letters From Colonial British Columbia* (City of Burnaby, 2002; p. 10).

The quote from L.A. Hamilton is taken from J.S. Matthews' *Early Vancouver* (Vol. 3, p. 183).

5: 'Those Who Own the Earth'

The *Vancouver Daily World* list of Vancouver's wealthiest taxpayers is taken from the December 31, 1889 issue (p. 1).

The figures about the nine buyers at the CPR Land Auction in Fairview comes from the *Vancouver News-Advertiser* (June 25, 1890), and the figure regarding absentee owners in DL 301 is taken from Graeme Wynn's "The Rise of Vancouver" in *Vancouver and Its Region* (UBC Press, 1992, p. 87).

6: Here Comes the Boom

A wealth of useful information regarding the boom of 1907–1913 comes from Robert A.J. MacDonald's "Business Leaders in Early Vancouver, 1886–1914" (PhD Thesis, UBC, 1977).

Much of the research regarding the Richard McBride Conservatives is taken from Martin Robin's *The Rush for Spoils: The Company Province 1871–1933* (McLelland and Stewart, 1972).

Property assessment information is taken from MacDonald, and from Patricia E. Roy's "A History of the Greater Vancouver Real Estate Bureau."

The *Province* quote about speculators comes from the June 2, 1906 issue, and the description of Dunbar's Point Grey purchases is taken from the November 20, 1906 issue.

Interlude: Real Estate and Race (Part I)

Information about the business activities of Chang Toy and the Sam Kee company are taken from Paul Yee's "Sam Kee: A Chinese Business in Early Vancouver" (*BC Studies*, Summer 1986, p. 69–70).

Data on the Chinese experience in early Vancouver come from Patricia E. Roy's *A White Man's Province* (UBC Press, 1989).

TERMINAL CITY

7: The Occupation

Details on Bob McEwan and the occupation of the second Hotel Vancouver are taken from "The Night War Vets Seized the Vancouver Hotel" (Claudia Cornwall, *The Tyee*, November 2006), and the January 23, 1946 issue of the *Vancouver Sun*.

8: Better

A host of information on the BHS and the homes it financed is taken from H. Peter Oberlander's *Housing a Nation: The Evolution of Canadian Housing Policy* (UBC, 1992), and "The Better Housing Scheme Bungalow In 1920 Vancouver: Wedding Economy And Aesthetics In The Craftsman Model" by Janadine Tyner (MA Thesis, UBC, 1990).

Statistics on rents and demographics are taken from the 1921 Census, and Donna McCririck's "Opportunity and the Workingman: A Study on Land Use Accessibility and the Growth of Blue Collar Suburbs in Early Vancouver" (MA Thesis, UBC, 1981).

The quote about discontented rent-payers is taken from the February 23, 1921 issue of the *BC Record*.

William Lyon Mackenzie King's comment about socialism is taken from Hansard (June 18, 1935, Vol. 4, p. 3773).

9: Welcome to the Jungle

Information on the life of Helena Gutteridge comes from Irene Howard's *The Struggle for Social Justice in British Columbia: Helena Gutteridge, the Unknown Reformer* (UBC Press, 1992).

Descriptions of the float homes and hobo jungles are taken from "Slums of the Waterfront" (CVA, City Clerk records, 27-D-5, file 17, 1939), and the Interim Report of the Special Council for Housing (CVA, City Clerk Records, 1938).

Description of a sheriff's eviction is taken from "Citizens in Action," (City Clerk's Series, Special Committee Meeting 1939, Vol. 69, p. 13, 334, 343).

Additional details on the hobo jungles are taken from Jill Wade's "Home or Homelessness? Marginal Housing Conditions in Vancouver 1886–1950", *Urban History Review*, (Vol. 25, No. 2, March 1997).

The quote on the housing crisis and Gutteridge's response come from the November 6, 1941 edition of the *Vancouver Daily News-Examiner*. Alderman H.L. Corey's response is taken from the November 7 edition.

Insight into the NPA's political tactics comes from Samuel Hays, "The Politics of Reform in Municipal Government in the Progressive Era," *Pacific Northwest Quarterly* (Vol. 55, No. 4, October 1964, p. 3–26).

The NPA advertisement in the *Vancouver Sun* is from December 11, 1939.

The *Province* quote about Helena Gutteridge's effect on city council is taken from the December 18, 1939 edition.

The 1957 interview with Gutteridge is taken from the March 8, 1957 edition of the *Pacific Tribune*.

10: **Empty**

Quotes from Andrew Haggart's presentation to City Council are taken from the October 6, 1942 edition of the *Vancouver Province*.

The story of George Reifel, Ross Lort, and the $1000 bill comes from Donald Luxton's *Building the West: The Architects of British Columbia* (Talonbooks, 2007).

The quote regarding vacant houses for sale (as well as the estimate of empty homes) is taken from the Jan 11, 1945 edition of the *Vancouver Sun*.

The "Why should a piece of empty real estate be sacrosanct?" editorial is taken from the December 27, 1944 edition of the *Vancouver Sun*.

11: **'Haunt of the Ragged'**

Information on slum clearance in Strathcona and the life of Gerald Sutton Brown is taken from: "The Place of the Poor: Poverty, Space, and the Politics of Representation in Downtown Vancouver 1950–1997" (Jeffrey D. Sommers, PhD Thesis, SFU, 2001), "Is Sutton Brown God? Planning Expertise and the Local State in Vancouver, 1952–73" (Will Langford, *BC Studies* 173, 2012), and "Freeway Planning and Protests in Vancouver 1954–1972" (Ken Mackenzie, MA Thesis, SFU, 1985).

Excerpts from Gerald Sutton Brown's speech to the Vancouver Rotary Club are taken from the October 9, 1953 edition of the *Vancouver Sun*.

Sutton Brown's pejorative remarks about Vancouver come from the April 25, 1952 edition of the *Vancouver Province*.

The Vancouver Board of Trade's plea to council for public money to revitalize downtown was found in *A Brief To City Council* (CVA Pamphlet 1951, Civic Bureau of the Vancouver Board of Trade, p. 1–2).

The description of Gerald Sutton Brown is taken from the December 11, 1959 edition of the *Vancouver Sun*.

The quote about a "spiral of ever-increasing dependency" is taken from the "Report of the Special Joint Commitee on Skidrow Problems" (CVA, Social Service Dept. 107-1-7).

The interview with the Salvation Army Major is taken from the November 10, 1952 edition of the *Province*.

Sutton Brown's quote about the "best interests of the city" comes from the April 22, 1958 edition of the *Vancouver Sun*.

Information on Project 200 and the protests it engendered is taken from "Freeway Planning and Protests in Vancouver 1954–1972" (Ken Mackenzie. MA Thesis. SFU. 1985), as well as "A Place for the Poor: Poverty, Space, and the Politics of Representation in Vancouver 1950–1997" (Jeffrey D. Somers, PhD Thesis, SFU, 2001).

Gerald Sutton Brown's speech on urban renewal was taken from "Urban Renewal: Municipal Organization and Policy," 21 (paper presented at the Fourth Session of the Canadian Mortgage and Housing Corporation Urban Renewal Seminar, 1959; file 11, 77-F-2, PRS 648, CVA).

Figures for the expropriation of Chinatown and Strathcona property are taken from the February 17, 1968 issue of the *Vancouver Sun*.

'CASTLES IN THE AIR'

13: Strata-fied

Allan Fotheringham's visit to Crescent View Apartments was reported in the June 22, 1973 edition of the *Vancouver Sun*.

"Castles in the Air" is from the February 11, 1966 edition of the *Vancouver Sun*.

Statistics on condo conversion rates in Vancouver come from Stanley Hamilton's "Condominium Conversion Regulations In British Columbia" (MA Thesis, UBC, 1987), p. 90.

Jack Poole's condo endorsement comes from the September 16, 1968 edition of the *Vancouver Sun*.

Jack Poole's complaints about developers, and his characterization of Daon as "small potatoes" both come from the December 28, 1974 edition of the *Vancouver Sun*.

The "Less than Rent!" debacle was reported in the November 18, 1972 edition of the *Sun*.

The complaints of NDP candidates Amy Dalgleish and John Stanton are taken from the November 22, 1972 edition of the *Vancouver Province*.

Miscellaneous details about Poole's life come from a profile by Gary Mason in the July 2, 2009 issue of *BC Business*.

14: There's No 'I' In Team

Invaluable information on the housing of Vancouver's low-income population is taken from Jill Wade's "Home or homelessness? Marginal housing in Vancouver, 1886–1950," *Urban History Review* 2 (1997), p. 19–29.

Useful context for the development of the False Creek waterfront are taken from Jacopo Miro's "Visions of False Creek: Urban Development and Industrial Decline in Vancouver" (MA Thesis, UVic, 2009), and Jeffrey D. Sommers' "A Place for the Poor: Poverty, Space, and the Politics of Representation in Downtown Vancouver 1950–1997," (PhD Thesis, SFU, 2001).

The assessment of Gerald Sutton Brown's dismissal comes from "A Guillotine Job," in the January 11, 1973 edition of the *Vancouver Province*.

Brian Calder's lambasting of TEAM candidates is taken from an October 3, 1968 interview with the *Sun*.

The description of False Creek's deplorable condition comes from the September 28, 1957 edition of the *Province*.

Art Phillips' development of Vancouver's new civic motto is taken from the November 7, 1969 edition of the *Vancouver Sun*.

15: "Lock, Stock and Carrall"

A wealth of useful information on the revitalization of Gastown comes from Michael Edema Leary-Owhin's *Exploring the Production of Urban Space* (Policy Press, 2016; p. 67–101).

Information on Larry Killam's career in Gastown is taken from the September 23, 1978 edition of the *Province*.

The Gary Bannerman profile of Killam is taken from the May 8, 1971 edition of the *Province*, and the *MacLean's* profile of Killam comes from the January 1971 issue.

Killam's quote about displacing pensioners comes from the September 3, 1969 edition of the *Sun*.

Patricia Kelly's Letter to the Editor is taken from the September 15, 1969 of the *Sun*.

Killam's attempts to discourage homosexual clientele in his buildings is explored in the May 8, 1971 issue of the *Province*.

16: Monster Houses

Information on the life of Larry Cudney is courtesy of his stepdaughter, Elizabeth Murphy, from an August 17, 2017 piece in the *Sun*.

The reference to Vancouver Specials as a "cancer" is taken from the March 13, 1984 edition of the *Sun*.

The opinion that Vancouver Specials are here to stay is taken from the April 7, 1978 edition of the *Sun*.

Mary McAlpine's analysis of the phenomenon comes from the January 20, 1978 issue of the *Sun*, Judy Lindsay's is taken from the November 13, 1979 edition, and Barbara Pettit's comes from the March 3, 1984 edition.

17: Rent Control (Part 1)

Copious amounts of information on the history of rent control in BC was taken from Celia Lazzarin's "Rent Control and Rent Decontrol in British Columbia: A Case Study of the Vancouver Rental Market 1974 to 1989" (MA Thesis, UBC, 1990).

The showdown in the Kitsilano High School auditorium was reported in the January 11, 1974 edition of the *Sun*.

Bruce Yorke's quotes are taken from his essay "The Tenant Movement in BC from 1968 to 1978" (Bruce Yorke, 1978, CVA AM1264).

Ernie Broome's complaint about a "Pandora's Box of ills" comes from the August 28, 1968 edition of the *Sun*. Bill Wallace's complaints are taken from a letter sent to the newspaper on April 24, 1969.

Herb Capozzi's comments about socialists in the Tenant's Union is taken from a speech before the Apartment and Rooming House Operators' Association, given in May of 1969.

Brian Calder's conflicting quotes from the *Sun* are taken from the April 6 and April 7, 1971 editions.

Pat McGeer, Harvey Schroeder, Emery Barnes, and Alex MacDonald's comments are taken from a transcript of debate in the BC Legislature (Hansard, April 8, 1974).

Linda Hossie's comments on ARP are taken from the November 16, 1979 issue of the *Sun*.

A frank assessment of *ARP* and Daon's exploitation of it is taken from Mary McAlpine's 'The Housing We Don't Need', in the January 20, 1978 edition of the *Vancouver Sun*, and Bruce Yorke's comments about *ARP* being a "license to print money" are taken from the April 18, 1977 issue of the *Sun*.

Walter Block's comments on slavery are taken from "Rand Paul's Mixed Heritage" (*New York Times*, January 25, 2014), and his remarks on the productivity of women and people of colour come from an address to the students of Loyola College (November 2008).

Jim Hewitt's comments come from an interview in the August 10th, 1983 issue of the *Sun*.

Robin Blencoe's comments are taken from a debate in the BC Legislature, (Hansard, April 9, 1984).

Interlude: Real Estate and Race (Part II)

Details about the life of David Lam, as well as relevant quotes, are taken from Reginald Roy's *David Lam: A Biography* (Douglas and MacIntyre, 1996).

RED

18: The Regatta

The initial story about the sale of The Regatta comes from the December 14, 1988 edition of the *Sun*.

Li's complaints about other condo developments is taken from the December 15 , 1988 edition of the *Sun*, and his eventual apology comes from the January 4, 1989 edition.

Statistics on Regatta units being resold comes from the March 30, 1989 issue of the *Sun*.

The comments from the *Chinatown News* are taken from the April 3, 1989 issue.

19: The Pacific Strategy

A large amount of research and statistics regarding the Pacific Strategy and the sale of the Expo Lands are taken from David Ley's *Millionaire Migrants: Trans-Pacific Life Lines* (UBC Press, 2010), Stan Persky's *Fantasy Government* (New Star Books, 1989), and from "Is Your City Being Sold Off to Global Elites?" (Paul Roberts, *Mother Jones*, May 2017).

Quotes from Karen O'Shannacery are taken from an interview with the author for the May, 2016 issue of *Megaphone* magazine.

The Pete McMartin quote about Mayor Harcourt's trip to Asia is taken from the March 6, 1985 edition of the *Sun*.

20: The Sale

The *Sun* quote about Victor Li comes from the December 17, 1988 edition.

The assessment of Peter Brown's character comes from an unnamed family friend, quoted in *Fleecing the Lamb: The Inside Story of the Vancouver Stock Exchange* (David Cruise and Alison Griffiths, Douglas and McIntyre, 1987).

Victor Li's interview with the *Sun* is taken from the February 25, 1989 issue.

Peter Toigo's complaint about Li Ka-Shing stealing the Expo Lands is taken from the July 16, 1988 edition of the *Sun*.

Jack Poole's "grave misgivings" come from the April 16, 1988 issue of the *Sun*.

Eric Downton's assessment of racism in the real estate market comes from the February 16, 1989 issue of the *Sun*.

Interlude: Real Estate and Race (Part III)

Information and statistics about the Business Investor Scheme and Chinese Immigration are taken from David Ley's *Millionaire Migrants* and Paul Roberts' article for *Mother Jones*.

21: The Coup

Gordon Campbell's comments about private industry being "the only way we change the city" are taken from the November 19, 1984 edition of the *Sun*.

An assessment of Campbell's personal and professional dealings — as well as all relevant quotes — are taken from Rafe Mair, *Georgia Straight*, May 30, 2007.

Calder's comments about the NPA's lack of "developer mentality" come from the September 27, 1985 edition of the *Sun*.

Harry Rankin's arguments about offshore speculation are taken from the December 19, 1988 issue of the *Sun*.

Donald Gutstein's comments about Campbell being a 'developer Mayor', and his assessment of Campbell's TEAM/Marathon conflict of interest come from the November 13, 1986 edition of the *Sun*, while Harry Rankin's fears of developers carving up the city are taken from the November 17, 1986 issue.

Alan Artibise's admission of the development industry's influence on "Future Growth, Future Shock," are taken from Katharyne Mitchell's "Conflicting geographies of democracy and the public sphere in Vancouver, BC" (*Transactions of the Institute of British Geographers*, 1996), and her book *Crossing the Neoliberal Line: Pacific Rim Migration and the Metropolis* (Temple University Press, 2004).

Statistics about the money raised by NPA fundraising dinners is taken from the November 5, 1990 edition of the *Sun*.

22: Concert

Information on the history of Concert Properties is taken from Rafe Mair's May 30, 2007 article in the *Georgia Straight*.

Gordon Campbell's quote about conflicts of interest with Brian Calder is taken from the November 13, 1986 edition of the *Vancouver Sun*. A breakdown of Campbell's many conflicts of interest is taken from journalist Russ Francis' September 4, 1993 editorial in the *Vancouver Sun*.

Brian Calder's business philosophy and thoughts on government intervention come from the March 5, 1994 edition of the *Sun*.

Libby Davies' complaints about Campbell's management style, and Jim Green's assessment of the VLC plan both come from the May 26, 1989 edition of the *Sun*.

Baker's comments on the VLC scandal are taken from the November 12, 1996 issue of the *Sun*.

Lionel Wazny's admission regarding Concert's hazy social purpose comes from the February 25, 1994 edition of the *Sun*.

Ken Georgetti's bragging about The Drake is taken from the October 1, 2010 issue of *VanMag*.

Interlude: A Brief History of Bob Rennie

Information on the life and career of Bob Rennie come from several sources, including "The Secret Passion of Bob Rennie" (*VanMag*, 2008).

Details on Rennie's presales to friends is taken from "Vancouver developers shutting out regular buyers with insider condo sales" (Kathy Tomlinson, *The Globe and Mail*, June 17, 2016).

23: Rent Control (Part II)

Details about the City Hall protest are taken from the December 20, 1989 edition of the *Sun*.

The rent control study comes from a report released by the city planning department, and was reported in the November 7, 1989 edition of the *Sun*. Additional rent control stats, and Brian Calder's claims about the apartment rental market come from the January 20, 1990 edition.

David Hulchanski's quote is taken from the March 31, 1990 edition of the *Sun*.

Walter Block's whining about socialism is taken from the January 18, 1990 edition of the *Sun*.

Conclusion

Jack Poole's meeting with developers, and Frank O'Brien's comments on the true nature of the Olympic bid, are taken from the June 2002 issue of *Western Investor*, and from "Developers are the Olympic Games' real winners" (Donald Gutstein, *Georgia Straight*, May 30, 2007).

Statistics on the explosion of home prices under Gordon Campbell are taken from data provided by the Greater Vancouver Real Estate Board (Residential Average Price Sales, 1977–2016).

Tsur Somerville's real estate connections were explored by Ian Young (*South China Morning Post*, March 18, 2015).

About the Author

JESSE DONALDSON is an author and journalist whose work has appeared in *VICE*, *The Tyee*, *The Calgary Herald*, the *WestEnder*, the *Vancouver Courier*, and many other places. His first book, *This Day In Vancouver*, was a finalist for the Bill Duthie Booksellers' Choice Award (BC Book Prizes). He currently lives near Mount Pleasant with Abbey, the world's best dog.